GEORGE
BEST
DOWN
UNDER

GEORGE BEST DOWN UNDER

by Lucas Gillard
with a contribution from
Jason Goldsmith

FAIRPLAY
PUBLISHING

First published in 2024 by Fair Play Publishing
PO Box 4101, Balgowlah Heights, NSW 2093, Australia

www.fairplaypublishing.com.au

ISBN: 978-1-925914-97-9
ISBN: 978-1-925914-98-6 (ePub)

© Lucas Gillard 2024 and Jason Goldsmith
The moral rights of the authors have been asserted.

All rights reserved. Except as permitted under the *Australian Copyright Act 1968* (for example, a fair dealing for the purposes of study, research, criticism or review), no part of this book may be reproduced, stored in a retrieval system, communicated or transmitted in any form or by any means without prior written permission from the Publisher.

Cover design and typesetting by Leslie Priestley

Cover photograph of George Best in Sydney 1983 from the Fair Play Collection.

Other photographs from the Fair Play Collection, Laurie Schwab Collection, or supplied by the authors.

All inquiries should be made to the Publisher via hello@fairplaypublishing.com.au

NATIONAL LIBRARY OF AUSTRALIA

A catalogue record of this book is available from the National Library of Australia.

Contents

Introduction 1

The Path to Greatness (1967) 7

Un-United (1975-1982) 16

Fed to the Lions (1983) 31

A Bit on the Side (1983) 44

The Belfast Swagman (1983) 52

The Inter Years (1984-1988) 59

Rats in the Ceiling (1989) 63

Law and Disorder (1990) 75

The Final Act (1991-2005) 81

George Best's Games In Australia

Bibliography and Related Sources

About the Authors

Introduction

There is no more iconic, haunted and hallowed figure in world football than George Best. Football came naturally to him as a skinny, shy boy from Bell's Bridge on the sprawling Cregagh Estate in East Belfast. While still a teen, he took his talents to Manchester United and exploded globally. He was awarded the Ballon d'Or in 1968 when his beloved Red Devils lifted the European Cup after his mesmerising goal broke the deadlock with Benfica in extra time.

He was a feted star who was the first to merge football with pop culture, creating a bridge between the virtuous icons of Sir Stanley Matthews and Sir Bobby Charlton, and the youth movement that was changing the world around them. Sir Bobby Charlton was many things, but with his lank combover and disciplined visage, he could never be 'cool'. George was different. He was the 'fifth Beatle', the dazzling playboy on and off the pitch and a man well and truly ahead of his time.

George Best died in 2005 due to a kidney infection that was the by-product of 35 years of heavy drinking into his middle age. To the public's incredulity and delight of the tabloids, his internal organs turned on him like many friends, lovers, managers and fans had over the years. As he was laid to rest in Belfast, the world wondered where it had all gone wrong for arguably the most deific talent in the game's history.

He never lost the passion for football that defined that boy in Cregagh who slept with a football and humiliated opponents on the estate for sport. Even as football forced him into second, third and fourth chances, each time in more remote locations, he could never give it up.

As his right knee swelled to the point of immobility, his skills became the plaything of emirs and the mega-rich in Southeast Asia. He still played for them because it was the only thing he ever wanted to do. In 1989, when Best was touring Australia for the third time at 43, his tour program proclaimed that "none ... surpassed and many argue, none measured up to Best". But washed up and on one working leg playing exhibition games in Tasmania and the outer suburbs of Melbourne, something had definitely gone wrong with Best's talent.

Ultimately Best the man could not measure up to Best the legend.

Today, Best is characterised in folklore and paeans on the Stretford End as combining three simple elements: precocious football ability, habitual drinking and a string of salacious affairs. All three are true to Best's character but are the consequences of an old and tired narrative on Best the man. Best drank himself to death because he had an illness that he openly admitted to an unsympathetic public as early as the 1980s. It was an illness that cost him his career at Old Trafford, forced him into his nomadic football life, consumed the life of his mother Anne (in 1978) and had no permanent cure. He tried therapy, detox, hypnotherapy, abstinence—once going as long as 14 months sober—and limitation. He went on Antabuse tablets orally and then had them implanted in his stomach. Nothing worked.

Unlike his linear portrayals on the terraces, Best was an extremely complex character. He had a genius intellect (his IQ was reportedly measured at 158), was fiercely combative, but also introverted and self-destructive. He could also rightly be defined as a misogynist who could be violent with his partners. There are parts of Best's character that are indefensible. And multiple cries for help from Best fell on deaf ears by a media and fan base hungry for scandal.

A George Best in the 2020s may have faced a more sympathetic media and support base. Backstops and support would come out of every corner of Old Trafford. He would be embraced for his candidness and adored for his media-untrained humour. But from the mid-70s onward when his career in the UK was over, he got none.

Best's drinking problems stemmed from his insatiable quest for greatness on the pitch and the distance that grew between greatness and reality for Manchester United in the years after their 1968 European Cup win. Best was only 22 then and the star player in a team facing imminent dissolution. Sir Matt Busby's powers waned, as did illustrious teammates Bobby Charlton, Denis Law and Paddy Crerand.

In the years following 1968, United signed poorly, managed the transition from Busby to assistant Wilf McGuinness poorly and turned the team over to Best without the supporting cast he needed. United wilted while Best's star was at its peak, and Best could not reconcile the decline with his quest for immortality. And he was constantly doing it all in the public eye. He received 10,500 letters a week from fans extolling him to be great. But he alone could not save United. "The old thrill of the game was gone," Best later reflected.

To fill the space, he turned to alcohol. Alcohol also filled a gaping hole in Best's personality. He was an introvert, and only two things allowed him to express himself publicly: drinking and football.

In times when he was sober, football was his only outlet for self-expression. Even when he was 'over the hill', Best revelled in beating opponents with his cunning, trying 40-yard chips and making opponents look amateur. But as biographer Duncan Hamilton

INTRODUCTION

put it, "The apparently brazen self-confidence was a front. Here was someone who could be as insecure as an infant."

Australia held a special significance for Best. His 1967 visit to the country with Manchester United was the first step on their path to his most significant achievement in the game, winning the European Cup. His second visit in 1983 was an opportunity for redemption from a historical low point for him.

In 1983, he battled depression, a final separation from his wife Angie, and another failed effort to rebuild his football career in Britain with Bournemouth.

But Best needed to keep going, and football was his only craft. So, he had to accept when the Brisbane Lions called with a short-term contract offer for the 1983 National Soccer League (NSL) season.

Sloppy modern reflections of Best's time in 1983 talk about a playboy party animal who cavorted around the country and barely lifted a toe on the pitch. Elements of the Australian media were desperate for the alcoholic to appear. Instead, they received a sober and circumspect George Best who had agreed to walk into purgatory, receive his penance and start turning his life around.

The George Best who alighted the Malaysian Airlines plane in Sydney in July 1983 was on the smallest upward curve after hitting one of many rock bottoms. Few in Australia had put the pieces together, but iconic football writer Andrew Dettre stumbled on a fitting and accurate symbol of what Best had become. In the short weeks before Best's arrival, Dettre decried great stars, namely Best, hawking their skills around the world instead of sliding gracefully into retirement:

"Now with all his once unparalleled talents dissipated and well into the veteran stages, comes what he must surely consider the rock bottom: Australia."

The erudite Dettre even invoked Irish playwright George Bernard Shaw:

"I don't know what Brisbane Lions really expect from George Best. I wouldn't like to guess how his visit will turn out. I hope they don't burn their fingers and that they get value for their investment. I'd love to also believe that Best has read some of Shaw's plays. If he has, he may be tempted to turn himself into a modern day Androcles and become the man who is curing the current ailments of the Lions."

In Shaw's play, the Christian Androcles pulls a thorn out of a lion's paw only to find that compassion repaid when he is to be fed to the same lion in the Colosseum. Best was in a similar position when he arrived in Australia—staring into the abyss, ready for judgement from the football world, and hoping for compassion from the Lions.

In the piece, Dettre cast his critical eye on what Best's life had become:

"I find it unbelievably sad that so many soccer greats follow in the footsteps of punch-drunk boxers: pick up bit parts in Hollywood, become bouncers in Vegas casinos, etc."

The amount of ire Dettre reserved for Best would be a portent for how the rest of the media would greet the former Ballon d'Or on his arrival in Sydney. Best's contemporary, Sir Bobby Charlton, also travelled the world post-retirement picking up guest contracts and playing in exhibition games, including two guest gigs in the National Soccer League (where Best would be playing). Neither appearance came with as much scorn as Best received.

Australia has always been a stomping ground for guest stars. Football is not Australia's most popular sport. While hundreds of thousands of Australian kids play football, and both the Socceroos and Matildas draw millions of eyeballs during tournaments, football has never been back-page news. And Australian clubs have always struggled to turn participation into mass spectating.

Generally speaking, the post-war migration to Australia boosted the country's focus and love of football, but largely (although not exclusively) within communities from continental Europe.

Inexplicably, not many migrants from the British Isles (the largest group of migrants) turned their generational passion for Manchester United, or Liverpool, or Celtic into active support for Australian club football. And that left Australian clubs in an awkward situation where people weren't coming … outside of dropping their kids off to play for one of the club's junior teams.

Every marketing trick and inducement was tried to get fans to embrace the local product in between getting up at 5 a.m. to watch Manchester United play (or to listen on the World Service).

The story of league football in Australia is the unassailable quest to turn the glimmers of interest in football as a sport into flames of passion for local clubs. Converting the 'private' Australian football fan—who has found it easier since 1992 to slide into love with teams in England or the homeland of their grandparents—into a terrace goer has forever been the holy grail.

Men like Best, as well as Bobby Charlton before him and Kevin Keegan, Alessandro Del Piero and countless others after him, represented a key to unlocking those dormant fans. The Brisbane Lions hoped that Best fans would explore what the Lions had to offer and, just maybe, stick around and support the club.

Sadly, this concept of casual-to-regular fan transference hasn't happened. While fans came for the big names, they generally didn't stick around for the smaller ones, leaving many guest contracts feeling hollow at the end.

Even now as A-League marquee players are mooted, they are met with a mixture of excitement (a chance to see them play in the flesh) and bemusement: is getting that player to play a couple of mediocre A-League games worth the effort?

The additional carrot in Best's day was the absence of readily available TV matches. To see Best play football *at all* was part of the allure of his guest contract. Today's fans have seen Marcus Rashford play on streaming TV every week, and his goals repeated

INTRODUCTION

on a loop on social media. Seeing Marcus Rashford play in the flesh has somewhat less uniqueness than it did when Best came to Australia in 1983.

Watching George Best playing football in 1983 at a suburban park was the only access many fans had to him. It was the closest you could get to seeing the 1968 European Cup final.

Best and Charlton's itinerant post-retirement activities share something major in common: neither man could give football up. But while Charlton became a wandering diplomat for the sport—fulfilling a duty of sorts to the game that made him—Best's lure to keep playing was something more personal.

Football was the only positive addiction in Best's life. His life had fallen around him but he needed to keep playing. He famously said:

"I'm sure I'll still be playing at some level or other when I'm a sixty-year-old granddaddy. When my professional career is over, I'll probably be kicking a ball around on a park pitch for a Sunday pub team just to get a game somewhere."

It is said that there was a plaque in the living room of Best's childhood house that read, "However far we wander, wherever we may roam, our thoughts will be turned, to those we love at home." But by this stage of Best's career, his wandering was a conscious effort to be removed from the dangers of home. To take himself away from the George Best tabloid persona, and just do what made him *feel* at home: play football.

According to Duncan Hamilton:

"The strain of being who he was—and living up to the preconceptions—left him at various stages afraid, confused, angry, profligate and paranoid."

But on the football pitch, even at the age of 37 with his top-flight career behind him, he could just be himself.

By mid-1983 he was off grog, but needed football more than ever, and the best offer on the table was from Brisbane Lions. Sure, money was a factor, but it wasn't the only one. Even though he had been declared bankrupt in the UK in late 1982, he wasn't short of money. He told the *News of the World*:

"I can still afford to travel first class and buy the best bottle of champagne, even though I know I can't afford to drink it."

George Best the human being was both warm, loving and tender but also cold, unapproachable and escapist. He was extremely shy, but also the life of the party. He was a perfectionist who was desperate to win but sabotaged his success. He was a fitness fanatic who decimated his fitness with drink. He was a family man who preferred the company of strangers.

He was a paradox of unique proportions, and he had so many skins that one wonders if even he knew which one fit best.

His visits to Australia brought dizzying highs but also all-time lows. He was both jeered and loved. He wooed crowds and alienated them.

He arrived as the biggest star in the universe in 1967 and left in 1990 as a supernova.

This book was compiled from a mixture of interviews with people involved with the players at the time, the players themselves in some cases, and with historians. Quotes from individuals are typically cited, but where the anecdotes captured in this book are provided uncited, the source preferred not to be named. These anecdotes were always cross-checked with other primary and secondary sources. Research on secondary sources was extensive, and these sources are cited when used except the authors' own earlier book on George Best (*Be My Guest*, Fair Play Publishing, 2021).

The Path to Greatness (1967)

George Best's first visit to Australia with Manchester United proved more fateful than anyone at the time realised. The promotional tour at the end of the 1967 title-winning season—the first for United since the 1958 Munich flight disaster—wasn't uncommon for European teams. What was special about this tour was just how much it set United on the path towards the ultimate prize: the 1968 European Cup.

Best was still a slip of a man aged 21 in 1967, but he was already being canonised as a legend. He had debuted four years earlier and had steadily wowed fans as he left defenders in his wake.

While Best was visiting Australia for the first time in 1967, his celebrity preceded him. He had followers and fans, and a network of football people that he had 'degrees of separation' from. While Manchester is a long way from Melbourne on both actual and football maps, Best had throughlines to players, coaches and supporters who themselves would make significant impacts on Australian football.

One former NSL player and Manchester United fan was present at one of Best's early standout performances in the red jersey. Cliff Pointer, who played 95 times in the NSL and hundreds more in the New South Wales First Division with Blacktown City, was at Stamford Bridge in 1964 to see the baby-faced Best up against an emerging Chelsea side.

While the Chelsea sides of manager Tommy Docherty—who would go on to play a significant role in Best's life—were pacey, innovative and built around young academy talents, there was a steel to them exemplified by fullback Ron 'Chopper' Harris. One isn't given the nickname 'Chopper' lightly, and it was famously bestowed on an 18-year-old Harris in 1963 while marking Stoke City's iconic Stanley Matthews. His tackling was so brutal (and iconoclastic to Matthews) that his own fans booed him.

It wasn't long before it was Best's turn to face Chopper. Cliff Pointer remembers:

"Ron Harris used to run a sweet shop down the road where I used to live. His nickname was 'Chopper' because nothing went past him without a leg missing. He was marking him that night and I'll never forget Best got the ball on the halfway line and beat him, almost stopped, and Harris recovered, and he beat him again and just from 10 or 15 metres inside the Chelsea half, he tried to chip the keeper from 40 yards out because he saw him off his line. Peter Bonetti was in goal for Chelsea in those days and he was very agile, but he didn't actually touch it, it landed on the bar and went over. In the press the next morning, Tommy Docherty the Chelsea manager said, 'tonight we saw the birth of a genius,' and he was spot on. Best player in the world by a mile."

Best was an overnight sensation for a Manchester United side still finding its feet after the Munich disaster five years earlier.

By 1967, something magical was happening in Manchester. Favourite sons Bobby Charlton and Nobby Stiles had brought their World Cup-winning mentality back to Sir Matt Busby's side for the 1966–67 season, and George Best the precocious talent was evolving into George Best the superstar.

Alongside the talismanic Best and World Cup winners was Scottish goal-machine Denis Law. The famed holy trinity of Best, Charlton and Law are today immortalised in statue form outside Old Trafford, and their domination was just getting started in 1966–67.

With 24 wins, 12 draws and only six losses, United tallied 60 points for the season to win the First Division title ahead of Nottingham Forest (56), Tottenham Hotspur (56) and Leeds United (55).

Leading the line was Law with 23 goals, and Charlton and Best, combined for 22 between them. Their reward for the title-winning season was a six-week, 12-game post-season tour of the United States, New Zealand and Australia, which kicked off just four days after winning the title.

Within the touring party were some new faces that Sir Matt Busby was eager to look at. While they had the First Division trophy in their cabinet, the European Cup that Sir Matt craved since the days of his 'babes' was going to take something extra.

Brian Kidd was yet to play a senior game for Manchester United, but he went on that tour for experience and as he put it, "to make up the numbers and give them lads a rest". The 17-year-old Kidd's inclusion on the tour may have started humbly, but it would evolve to be something no one could have anticipated. Kidd had been in Turkey with the England youth team, only arriving back in England to fly out on the tour the next day.

Best turned 21 on that tour in San Francisco, and in his 2001 autobiography *Blessed*, he claimed that he celebrated his birthday at a British pub called the Edinburgh Castle, having fish and chips and a couple of beers with his friend Dave Sadler.

They started the tour in Los Angeles with a 3–1 loss to Benfica, followed by a 4–2 loss to Dundee United in San Francisco. Their domestic form wasn't translating onto American pitches, which may not seem an issue in 'meaningless' friendlies, but on some level, it was bothering Busby.

THE PATH TO GREATNESS (1967)

On the long flight from the US to New Zealand, Busby must have soul-searched, because United went undefeated for the rest of the tour. Indeed, his solution was to pull a rabbit out of a hat: and that rabbit was young squad member Brian Kidd.

Kidd remembers New Zealand vividly, and it was in Auckland that Busby told the boys to think big and dream of becoming the first English team to lift the European Cup.

"We hadn't played well, we hadn't done ourselves justice in America, when we get to New Zealand, I think it might have been Auckland first, when we get there, we went training in a park-like setting. Sir Matt sat us all down and said, 'Right, what's happened in America is not good enough, we start preparing now for the European Cup.'"

Busby wasn't happy with the way the team had performed in America. According to Kidd, "Sir Matt said, 'Right, nose to the grindstone, we start preparing right now!'"

New Zealand would bear the brunt of United's new steely resolve, with United winning 8–1 against an Invitational XI in Auckland and then thumping the New Zealand national team 11–0 in Christchurch. Best scored a brace on the North Island and another two on the South. The 11–0 result still stands as United's biggest ever overseas win.

From New Zealand, the Red Devils travelled to Australia where they would play eight games in five states in 24 days, scoring 33 goals, conceding only three and playing in front of just under 200,000 people.

By Australian crowd standards, the tour was seismic and highlighted just how big a drawcard the 'big' British clubs could be in the country. This was a massive club, with massive names, shaking dormant Australian football fans onto a paid seat.

According to the *Sydney Morning Herald*, Manchester United were being paid the modest fee of only $2,000 per game on their eight-game tour, with the Australian Soccer Federation inviting a cigarette company to help foot the bill. The insert in the official program reads:

"W.D. & H.O. WILLS, the makers of Craven Filter cigarettes in association with the Australian Soccer Federation have brought to Australia the internationally famous English Soccer Team MANCHESTER UNITED to compete against Australian Soccer Teams in a series of matches that will provide soccer fans the opportunity of seeing this world-renowned team in action."

Other sections of the official program for the 1967 tour could have been written by one of the thousands of young girls and boys who stalked Best outside the Old Trafford change rooms, but they were probably penned by veteran football journalist Andrew Dettre who put his pseudonym 'Paul Dean' to the profile of Bobby Charlton.

The piece on Best includes:

"His ability still knows no bounds. A colourfully modern character, he has a 'with it' taste in clothes and a Beatle haircut."

It continues:

"The sight of Best's frail looking figure conjuring the ball away from a rival defender with magic dexterity is enough to send any soccer fan away from the ground bubbling with excitement."

It also includes a quote from the then 21-year-old Best:

"When I'm on the field, nothing gives me more pleasure than making a fool out of somebody."

If Best had to take studs of players like Chopper Harris, he was also going to leave them and the crowds certain who was the better player.

Best was already an icon, and he dazzled Australian fans. One might think that a teenage Brian Kidd would be intimidated by the prospect of joining the champion team led by Busby and including Charlton, Law and Best, but that was not the case.

"It wasn't daunting because we'd gone to United as apprentices at 15. The way them senior players, not just looked after you, how they gave you principles and the desire, was what Manchester United was all about. I was only then 17, coming up to 18, so if we went to any reception dinners, there was always a taxi waiting for me to get me back early.

"It gave the senior players a bit of downtime, with me being the youngest just making the numbers up. It was absolutely fantastic. I can't thank them enough, the way they looked after me. It was for Sir Matt, so simple what it meant to be Manchester United, how you had to conduct yourself, your manners, he was like your Mum and Dad really."

United kicked off the Australian leg of their world tour at the Brisbane Exhibition Ground against Queensland in convincing fashion. They had a 7–0 win in front of a massive crowd for the times of 30,000. Such was their dominance they could have scored plenty more but Queensland goalkeeper Ross Kelly was recognised as player of the match due to some outstanding saves.

George Best scored a goal in each half, Bobby Charlton and John Aston two each, and Noel Cantwell one. The press were gushing in their praise of Charlton and Best:

"Charlton and Best repeatedly had the defenders nonplussed with brilliant ball control and sharp shooting."

The George Best show continued in the next game as Manchester United played a very strong New South Wales Representative XI in front of 25,000 fans.

It was New South Wales who got on the front foot early, making goalkeeper Alex Stepney work in the early stages before the gap in talent was exposed. Best scored two of United's three in their 3–0 win, with all the goals coming in the first half.

His silky skills were on display with his first via a narrow angle and his second after a characteristic dribble around two defenders before slotting it home. The *Sydney*

THE PATH TO GREATNESS (1967)

Morning Herald was glowing in their praise:

"Appearing all over the ground to spring away with the ball was that extraordinary right-winger Best. The body-swerve of the 21-year-old Irish international and his marvellous gift of controlled unpredictability had the Australians treading on ice."

The game petered out in the second half after Denis Law clashed with Socceroo Ron Giles. Giles came off second best and was taken to hospital with a broken jaw.

His injury was such that the part-time footballer was set to miss six weeks of work, but it was reported in *Soccer News* that the Manchester United players did a "whip around" and raised $500 for him. Sir Matt Busby approached New South Wales officials with the money, and Denis Law was a contributor.

In Sydney that night to watch Best was another famous football name, and one whose life would intersect with Best multiple times in both Australia and the UK.

David Jack's (the third of his name) lineage is legendary. He shares a paternal bloodline with Bob Jack—the legendary Edwardian player with Bolton and Plymouth. David Jack (the first) also became a legend with Bolton and had a record British transfer fee twice, becoming the first five-figure transfer when he joined Herbert Chapman's Arsenal in 1928. David Jack (the second) was a football writer who went on to chair the English Football Writers Association, and he was a News of the World editor's coin-toss away from sitting on the plane that fatefully crashed in Munich in 1958 with the United squad (he was sent to cover another game instead).

While Jack covered the Greater Manchester clubs in the mid-1960s, his son, David (the third), idolised the transcendent George Best before immigrating with his parents to Sydney. David (the second) went on to help pioneer football writing in Australia, while David the third trialled with Manchester United at the end of his hero Best's time there, before returning to a successful career in the NSW State League with Manly-Warringah. But his highlight would come over a decade later when he shared a pitch with George Best in a State match against Dee Why.

David Jack III, who lived in Manchester from the ages of four and 11 while his dad did the Lancashire beat, saw Best score his first goal for United in his second game against Burnley in a 5-1 win:

"I've always remembered that and it's funny that I played in a game where he probably scored one of his last goals."

Jack, the teenager, idolised Best and watched his early career at close quarters while following his father's work. But a hammer blow fell in early 1967 when he was forced to leave his United behind when his family emigrated to Australia.

"I didn't want to leave [for Australia]," Jack says. "I was a mad United fan and I couldn't leave them behind. [But] We left England in March 1967."

Thankfully for Jack, he wouldn't have to wait too long to see United again.

"Best scored a couple of amazing goals. Two games in Sydney—one was a Wednesday night game and it was pouring with rain—but he scored a goal from a short corner where he beat three or four players and just smashed it in. Incredible stuff. But funnily enough, I later played with the guy who was marking him. An old Australian player named Cliff van Blerk. He played a couple of games for Australia. But I then played with him at Western Suburbs and he was a funny bloke. And he'd always tell me about George Best, saying 'I shouldn't look so old but George Best took ten years off my life that day at the Sydney Showgrounds.'"

The third game was Manchester United's only blemish of the tour when they drew 1-1 with Victoria at Olympic Park. To put the gravity of this result into context, this preview of the game the day before ran in *The Age*:

"Manchester United, the greatest soccer team to visit Australia, should provide a breathtaking display of power and ball control when it clashes with Victoria at Olympic Park tomorrow. Victoria has no chance whatsoever of winning, or even drawing against Matt Busby's 'Red Devils'—$2 million worth of talent. The only question about tomorrow's game is how many goals will Manchester United score and how brilliant will they be?"

Australian football publication *Soccer News* had their own faulty crystal ball:

"For no one even in their wildest dreams can visualise Victoria winning or breaking even. Not even the most one-eyed Victorian soccer fan would think otherwise."

A Bobby Charlton goal in the early stages was equalled when David Sadler headed into the wrong net for an own goal. The Victorians were lauded as heroes and their herculean performance was reported as such in the *Soccer News* headline:

"VICTORIA, YOU DID US PROUD".

It continued:

"Today we pay tribute to eleven gallant men—the Victorian team who matched Manchester United stride for stride at Olympic Park on Sunday.

"The 1-1 draw was no fluke. It came as a result of sheer determination and courage from the finest team this State has produced in its 60 years of football."

Manchester United's cramped schedule meant they then flew from Melbourne to Newcastle on the evening of the game to face a Northern New South Wales rep side.

An often-overlooked part of United's rebuild after the Munich disaster is that they just had to continue to get onto planes. Sir Bobby Charlton, a survivor at Munich, spent much of his retirement on planes flying around for exhibition games—including playing twice in Australia's NSL. His only option, along with the club's, was to grit his teeth and hope for the best.

According to Kidd, the vast expanse of Australia didn't help with their anxiety in the air.

"All that flying wasn't a good thing for us [after Munich]."

The team's arrival in Newcastle after 90 minutes in Melbourne has gone down in

United folklore. Newcastle Airport staff forgot the team was coming and had closed the airport. The players had to help unload their suitcases from the plane with the help of a couple of torches.

On a boggy pitch at the Newcastle Sports Ground, they finished 3-0 winners with young Brian Kidd scoring twice and George Best adding the third. That took Best's Australian tally to five goals in four games. Despite getting on the goal sheet, the *Sydney Morning Herald* was somewhat subdued in their praise:

"Manchester's right-winger George Best was deceptive and non-stop in his effort but again carried the ball too far on occasions."

But the Newcastle match was more about Brian Kidd than Best. This was Kidd's breakthrough game, proving to his manager that he was more than capable of impressing against grown men. It was a point later rammed home in style in the 1968 European Cup final when Kidd scored United's third goal in extra time to take the game away from Benfica.

A new, supreme United side was taking shape on Australian soil. And their ringleader, George Best, was about to rewrite the record books.

The United boys were rewarded after the Newcastle match with some time off back in Sydney. Their next game at the Sydney Showgrounds was six days later.

Enjoy Sydney they did with days spent around Coogee Beach, and nights around the entertainment district of Kings Cross. After winning the 1966-67 English First Division and being on tour almost straight away, it was really the first time they could enjoy themselves.

For young Brian Kidd, it was like another world, and it is the cuisine that he remembers the most:

"When we got to Sydney, they were serving us Oysters Mornay and with me being a lad from Collyhurst, I thought, what's Oysters Mornay? It was really funny with some of them lads like Paddy Credlin all laughing at me. The lads had a super time, socially as well as we were well looked after."

United prevailed again against New South Wales 3-1. A large crowd saw Bobby Charlton score twice and Bill Foulkes once in front of young starry-eyed David Jack. New South Wales captain and Socceroo Pat Hughes scored late for the hosts. It was a kind of reunion for Hughes, who had been a youth-level teammate of United's Pat Crerand back in Scotland.

After enjoying the spoils and oysters of Sydney Harbour, United were booked to return to Melbourne for a revenge match against Victoria, this time with Denis Law back in the side. The fawning press that praised Victoria's earlier 1-1 draw seemed to lose their edge with the news of Law's return. The headline screamed:

"MURDER; That's what it could be".

It continued:

"When you see Manchester United's line-up for their final game in Victoria, your eyes will pop out. The Red Devils have chosen their strongest possible side to 'put Victoria in their place'."

And their Hollywood predictions proved right. Law was on the scoresheet twice as the tourists completed a 4-0 rout. After an opening own goal, it was George Best who stole the show. He created both of Law's goals and scored one himself after a remarkable solo dribbling effort. *The Age* reported:

"Best scored Manchester United's third goal in the 70th minute with a sterling shot after a fine solo effort which left Victoria's defenders completely startled."

One might assume that after their successful run, Manchester United had earned the right to take the foot off the pedal with just two tour games remaining. But with Sir Matt Busby in charge, that was not likely to happen, as Brian Kidd remembers:

"Under Sir Matt, no matter what the game, be it a friendly game, an exhibition game, a Cup game or a League game, we had to uphold the standard of Manchester United."

That suited the ultra-competitive Best to a tee. But at Kensington Oval in Adelaide for the penultimate game, it was Kidd who stole the show. After goals to Charlton and Law, Kidd scored the last three in a 5-1 win.

United's final game on the tour finished with the same scoreline as the first, this time a 7-0 romp over Western Australia in front of 20,000 at the WACA ground. The visitors managed the result with only 10 men for most of the game after Denis Law was sent off for bad language at the 30-minute mark. But being a player up was unlikely to turn the tide for WA, as they were already 3-0 down when it happened.

This was George Best's greatest game of the tour. Not only did he score three, but he managed to create two more as well. Overall, Best scored nine of United's 33 goals on tour, as well as having just as many assists and multiple chances. He was at the peak of his powers, and Brian Kidd reflects on what a champion Best was at that time.

"In them days they could hack you down then, it was a given, and they all tried it with George. The thing was, and all of the greatest defenders would tell you how good George was. They could get near him, but he was so brave, he would always go back for more. If he'd lose the ball, he would go back to retain it. His work ethic on the defensive side was super, because that was demanded of him from Sir Matt."

It was a perspective on Best that Cliff van Blerk could relate to. Best had torn into the Australian sides with his usual mix of flair, trickery and team ethic. Whether it was an exhibition game in Newcastle, or a European Cup final at Wembley, Best gave all of himself to the game.

The 1967 Manchester United tour of Australia certainly made an impression. It inspired thousands of Australian fans, both United fan boys and casual fans alike. It introduced a young giant-slayer named Brian Kidd to the world. And it also created fond memories for United's star, George Best. Australia resonated with him as a warm and welcoming place. When Best returned in 1983, he told Michael Parkinson in an interview:

"I haven't been here since 1967 and I had a wonderful time then, and I've met a lot of old friends and the people have been tremendous."

And while he was being generous in 1983, his memories of 1967 never left him. He was a legend in the making and on the cusp of greatness with the greatest United team ever assembled. After Australia, he would soon become one of football's immortals, but it would take a few 'lifetimes' before he could return.

Un-United (1975-1982)

The epic 1967–68 season that started in Australia and ended with the European Cup and a Ballon d'Or for Best was undoubtedly the summit of Best's football career. In the years after these triumphs, it has also symbolised the first step in both United and Best's descent.

Best's illustrious teammates like Charlton, Law, Stiles and Crerand passed their peaks just as Best was coming into his, and the pressure of becoming United's marquee player began to take a toll on him. Legend and father figure Sir Matt Busby was also at an age where he needed to hand over the team, and a series of managerial missteps, failed signings and poor planning overall saw United go from European Champions to mid-table fodder.

Despite Best topping the United goal-scoring from 1969–1972, the team finished eighth in all three seasons.

The management of the club was passed from Busby (after 24 years) to assistant Wilf McGuiness in 1969. He lasted half a season before Busby returned for an emergency second half. Leicester City's Frank O'Farrell was handpicked by Busby for the 1971 season which started brightly before his star man, one George Best, disappeared for a month and the tide turned.

A desperate O'Farrell transfer listed Best for a reported £300,000 fee (more than double United's then record signing), but by then Best's reputation preceded him and no team was willing to flinch.

After 1968, Best had chosen alcohol to medicate his growing anxiety over the plight of his team. It was self-destructive and counterintuitive, but on the pitch, he could no longer find the joy and excitement to match the peaks of 1968.

He began to spend more time in his Manchester nightclub than on the training pitch. His media persona as a playboy and pop idol took over, and stories of his drinking, womanising and absenteeism became sport for the media. In 1972 when his boot sponsorship deal with Stylo was taken from him and given to Kevin Keegan, one critic described Keegan as "not fit to lace Best's drinks".

UN-UNITED (1975-1982)

Best was off the rails so often that he was barely on them. In *Blessed*, he talks of this time:

"I was getting away with it because of who I was, or because of who my alter ego was."

Best had become a character that he could summon and use as an excuse to not think about football.

Best also 'retired' while on a holiday in Marbella in May 1972. When the dust settled on his decision, he saw it as a siesta (12 days it had been) and Best returned for the 72–73 season. O'Farrell had been sacked after 18 months and replaced by former Chelsea and Scotland manager Tommy 'Doc' Docherty.

Docherty was a Scotland international who got his start at Celtic before having an illustrious career at Preston North End playing alongside the legendary Tom Finney. As a junior at Celtic, he worked with venerable coach Jimmy Hogan whose progressive passing philosophy had inspired football across Central and Eastern Europe in the interwar years. The Mighty Magyars trace their lineage to the teachings of Hogan, and Docherty is considered among his many protégés.

Docherty got his start in management with Chelsea, and he took them from a Second-Division side to a League Cup trophy and an FA Cup final appearance. He resigned from Chelsea in 1967 before drifting across leagues and continents, then picking up the Scotland job and steering them towards qualification for the 1974 World Cup—a qualification they ultimately completed after his departure.

Midway through 1972, Docherty joined Manchester United, who were desperate to right the ship after drifting towards relegation under O'Farrell.

Best's early experiences with Docherty were positive, with Docherty declaring him off limits to other clubs, but when the reality of Best's attitude became clear he too was ready to move him on. He put Best back on the transfer list but, like before, no one was willing to take the risk.

Best was coaxed into returning to both football and United by Docherty's right-hand man, former teammate Paddy Crerand. While Best worked on regaining his fitness, he also made a decision off the field that would come back to haunt him: he opened an upscale wine bar and nightclub called *Slack Alice*.

Best claims he had a gentleman's agreement with Docherty that any training sessions missed would be retaken at his own convenience, often with Crerand in the afternoon. But opening a nightclub and fronting it for his clientele proved too seductive for Best. United weren't gelling as a team on the pitch, he wasn't yet back to full fitness, and at nights he had access to unlimited alcohol.

Best's Manchester United career was ended for him in 1974 when he was sacked by Docherty.

His United death knell came after an ill-fated Cup tie against Plymouth Argyle.

Best's habits of disappearing for days were legendary by now, but he was offered a career lifeline by Docherty in the days leading up to the Cup tie against lower-league Plymouth. Best accepted the offer in good faith and knuckled down to train and get back to an acceptable fitness level. In the week before the game, he missed one morning session, but believed he had paid a penance with an afternoon session. Docherty made nothing of the missed session, and Best eagerly anticipated kick-off.

What happened next drove a stake into Best's heart. According to legendary journalist Hugh McIlvanney:

"Shortly before the kick-off (it had to be then, because Best never arrived early) he was called into the referee's room and told by Docherty that he would not be playing. He tried to remonstrate, but Docherty was adamant."

Best recalled the incident as all but stamping his papers:

"When he and Paddy Crerand left me, I sat in that room and cried my eyes out ... Then after the match I went up into the empty stands and sat on my own for about an hour. I knew I had ceased to be a part of Manchester United and it was a desperate feeling."

In *Blessed*, Best identifies the root of his feud with Docherty. Best could almost accept the decision not to select him for the Cup game, but it was what Docherty told reporters that stuck with him.

"What annoyed me most was that Docherty told the press that I had turned up for the game drunk and with a girl on my arm, which was absolute rubbish. I never turned up drunk for a United game and I've certainly never reported to the dressing room with a girl."

Best also concedes:

"I've worked with Doc at dinners. I think he is a funny man. But I also think he can be a bullshitter."

When Docherty said goodbye to Best for good, he told the press:

"Bringing him back was a disaster. He was more trouble than he was worth."

United dragged their heels for 18 months in granting Best a free transfer, and when they did, Best conspired to collect his papers on a Sunday to be as inconvenient as possible for Docherty.

"I hated him so much I didn't even want to go there," he said. "The only reason I did was because I knew it was killing him to have to get up on a Sunday morning to go in."

Best's feud with Docherty would be played out publicly in Australia nine years later.

United were relegated at the end of 1974 after 36 years in the top-flight competition. Ironically, United legend Denis Law scored the final day winner for Manchester City in a 1-0 win that was a humiliating nail in the coffin of United's wretched year. Law had been released by Docherty the previous season.

Best's own sacking from United sparked his move into itinerant football labouring.

His heart belonged to United and he couldn't see himself playing properly for a rival despite offers from England and abroad.

His first move away from Old Trafford was a little less exotic than his future ones: it was to Southern League Division One North's Dunstable Town. In the bleak period where he wasn't playing for United but wasn't yet released by them, an old United friend, Barry Fry, visited Best in his Manchester nightclub with a peculiar offer.

Dunstable Town's crowds were small—almost so small they could have been for their reserve team—but their new manager Barry Fry had an idea. Fry had apprenticed at United with Best before injuries curtailed his playing career. And Best was looking for a place to play.

It was up to Fry then to convince the man who held Best's registration: Tommy Docherty. Eventually, through clever bargaining, some heartstring tugs and some potential funds being available to United, Docherty relented and offered the United Reserves as an opponent for an unlikely exhibition game.

On August 5, 1974, Best ran out for Dunstable Town in front of between 3,000 and 10,000 fans, depending on who you listen to. Whatever the figure was, it was certainly a fair improvement on their regular two-figure crowds. The amazing part of that game was that Best wasn't the only marquee on the pitch. Fry had also convinced former England star Jeff Astle to join the club in the League that season.

Best was mobbed after the 3–2 win as the crowd descended onto the pitch, and his temporary club were thrilled.

A week later, Cork City were in town for another exhibition game, and Best didn't disappoint. Despite showing up late due to an "auto malfunction", he put on another show. After Best's appearances, Dunstable Town started pulling crowds in the three- and four-figure region and were promoted at the end of that season, with Astle scoring 34 times.

A switch might have flicked for Best on those first exhibition nights, as he could see the power of his football brand on show. While he was only paid (reportedly) £200 per game (some of which he gave back to the club), it seemed there could be a big cachet for club owners globally if George Best appeared on their pitch.

Later in life, he would make guest appearances for Fry at Barnet and Maidstone, as the network he built in football could always be relied on to offer Best another contract, big or small. Wherever Best went, crowds followed.

His first move abroad in 1974 piqued his interest in turning his talent into a marketable product to support his lifestyle. He picked up a massive offer of £11,000 for six matches with the Jewish Guild in Johannesburg—a fee reportedly the equivalent of 35 First Division matches.

He then got a gig at Stockport County who more than quadrupled their gate when he arrived. Best scored in his first game for the Fourth Division side outside of

Manchester in a 1-1 friendly against top-division team, Stoke City. He also scored in his League debut, a win against Swansea City, but only appeared twice more after that. After Best's appearances, the season didn't quite go to plan for 'The Hatters' who went on a slide and had to reapply for admission to the League.

He then stopped by Cork City on his way to his first of many contracts in the North American Soccer League (NASL), starting with the LA Aztecs.

In 1976, he returned to England to play a full season for Bobby Moore and Rodney Marsh's Fulham in the second tier. There he more than doubled attendances from four figures, and he had 21,000 against Bristol Rovers for his debut. The Aztecs ostensibly loaned Best to Fulham, as the NASL season didn't clash too heavily with the English League season. Best expressed in an old interview aired on the Fulham supporter's podcast *Fulhamish* that an appeal of the NASL was it included opportunities to play in both the US and UK seasons every year. And the Aztecs would be compensated for the parts of the NASL season that clashed with Fulham's.

Fulham was as close to an elite regular club football that Best would get after Manchester United. He was still near the peak of his powers and indeed scored on his debut for Fulham. His second game for the club reportedly drew 25,000 fans to Craven Cottage.

A couple of seasons earlier as his United contract was dissolving, Best was close to joining Chelsea, but they baulked at his contract requests at the last minute. He was no stranger to West London and owned property near there. Later in life, he was a regular at a pub just off King's Road. In 1976, he finally got to make his move to West London, having fun and playing exciting football.

While Fulham were (only) a Second-Division side, his early period at Fulham was so inspiring in West London that the club, who obviously disliked puns, printed t-shirts for him that said, 'Georgie gets them going'.

The peak George Best moment occurred at home against Hereford United in front of the TV cameras. A jovial Best tackled teammate Rodney Marsh to win the ball off him, only to have Marsh return the challenge. Even the referee was chuckling to himself as Fulham won 4-1.

He played 42 games for Fulham and scored eight times over a couple of seasons, but the myth of Best is still uttered today at Craven Cottage. Like at most places he played, the lack of TV evidence has allowed terrace memories to become facts and part of the Legend of Best.

His chip goal away for Fulham in the League Cup at Peterborough is often cited as the greatest ever witnessed at London Road. Best also scored in a 3-1 win against bitter rivals Chelsea (still featuring Chopper Harris) in front of 29,000 in a win that is still invoked today.

Crowds varied throughout the year in a season that was up and down on and off the pitch. Fulham only finished mid-table, but the season is still remembered fondly at 'The Cottage'.

Best and Marsh were having so much fun together at Fulham that Best claims in Blessed he and Marsh were approached to release a record together. "But I can't sing," Best protested, which the record company took as a "no". It's a protest that Best should have reflected upon when he was next asked the question much later.

While at Fulham, Best was invited yet again to join Danny Blanchflower's Northern Ireland side, and he appeared in the apocryphal qualifier against Johan Cruyff and the Netherlands team in Rotterdam in 1976. He famously is said to have nutmegged Cruyff, allegedly aggrieved after Madame Tussauds had replaced their Best figurine in London with one of Cruyff. Another account is that he was put out by journalist Bill Elliott implying that Cruyff was the better player, and he offered to nutmeg him to prove otherwise. It is said that he succeeded after five minutes and raised his fist in the air in triumph. Northern Ireland managed a 2–2 draw that night against one of the world's best teams.

While it's debated whether this nutmeg occurred, it hardly mattered at the time. Best had a blinder against the eventual World Cup finalists. Best's next couple of games for his national team were less memorable (losses to Belgium and then the Dutch again) and, sadly, they would be his last turnout for his national side. However, for as long as Best played semi-competitive football around the world, his name would be continuously linked with a recall.

Much like his career with the national team, his time at Fulham ended with more questions than answers, and it was punctuated in the middle by a shocking drink-driving accident that left him with a shattered shoulder blade and severe cuts to his face. Best returned to the field five weeks later but it took a long time for him to regain feeling in his arm. And his heavy drinking habit returned. It would follow him like his shadow as he moved on to the next phase of his American odyssey.

Years later, wife Angie reflected on America being the best possible place for Best, but that his frequent returns to the UK—especially the Fulham years—often brought new bouts of alcoholism with them.

"George changed the minute he got off the plane from America. We were just an anonymous couple in California but here [in London] he was famous ... He became introverted with the oppression London put on him. He started to walk with a stoop, his facial expression changed."

Stooped and forlorn, Best returned to America and kept the circus rolling with the Aztecs and then with the Fort Lauderdale Strikers. He was scoring goals and attracting fans, but also, sadly, courting controversy. In 1979, the Strikers made the unusual move of offering a statement to the press about Best's break-up (not for the last time) with his wife, Angela. The Strikers' spokesman more than crossed a line with this not quite paint-by-numbers statement:

"George keeps getting around with different beautiful girls and then, combined with his all-night drinking sessions, broke Angela's heart. I really think she still loves him."

The NASL loved controversy, and George provided it in spades. He provided memorable goals and even more memorable gossip.

Around this time, Best started working with a young player manager and former Hibernian youth product, Bill McMurdo. Together they established the George Best Management Company as a vehicle for Best to attract an income from pick-up games around the world. It was a lucrative venture for both men that spanned three decades, and it underpinned a friendship and fraternal bond between the two.

McMurdo had started working in football promotions in the mid-1970s, adding players to his books. Best was one of his first clients, along with Rangers' Derek Johnson.

He ultimately pioneered the infamous move of Mo Johnston to Rangers from Celtic (via Nantes) and continues to manage players around the world, including more recently Melbourne Victory's former bit-part Matias Sanchez. But in the late 1970s and early 80s, McMurdo had his hands full with George Best.

In 1980, Best joined Hibernian and became—according to folklore—Britain's best-paid player. He was in between gigs in America and was in England to play in Bobby Robson's testimonial match in Ipswich. By chance, Hibernian were looking for a celebrity to hand over a cheque for £1,000 to the winner of a prize at half-time in a League game. McMurdo suggested his client Best, who obliged, and then dutifully flew up to Edinburgh.

Sometime after the match, 'Hibs' chairman, Tom Hart, was questioned by reporters who had put two and two together and made five:

"Mr Hart, is it true Hibs are going to sign George Best?"

"No, George is here on a promotional exercise," Hart responded.

"Is that because you can't afford him?"

Hart's response brought the house down. "Oh, is that fucking right? I'll tell you what, George will sign for Hibs and the Hart family will pay the salary."

McMurdo was rightfully taken aback. Best had just signed with San Jose in America.

So, Tom Hart journeyed down to Ipswich to take in the Bobby Robson testimonial and make Best an offer he couldn't refuse. McMurdo intercepted Best after the match to let his client know what was coming.

"Do you fancy playing in Scotland?" he asked.

"What about America?" Best replied.

"Look, I can get out of that," was McMurdo's advice.

After a £2,500-per-game offer followed, Best indeed could not refuse. Old firm players at that time were on around £400 a week. Best could make more than ten times that on an average week that contained two matches. Hibs were rewarded with 16,000 fans at Best's debut against St Mirren: a bit of an upgrade on their 9,000 average!

But his return to British League football didn't last long—17 games and three goals, to be precise. Best went walkabout, and Hibernian had little choice but to void his contract. It was another in a growing line of disappointments for clubs who signed Best. His cycle was now very well defined. He could be trusted for early appearances and the commercial boosts that provided, but he was not going to be around to score the winner in a Cup final.

Best's relationship with football was becoming increasingly casual. He was drawn to big games, but quickly lost interest and focus.

It was at this time that Best started to publicly admit he was an alcoholic. On his dumping from the Edinburgh club, he told the media:

"Hibs had no option but to get rid of me. I've let everybody down so badly that there can be no excuses. Now I must get away and hope I can lick the problem of alcohol."

The exit from Hibernian also cost him a chance of joining his national team's tour of Australia. The Northern Irishmen visited in June 1980, getting two wins and a draw against Rudi Gutendorf's Socceroos. In the months before the tour, the chairman of the Northern Irish FA told *Soccer Action* that Best's inclusion on the tour "looks certain". But like all things related to George Best, nothing could ever be certain.

And in 1981 with qualification for the Spain '82 World Cup looking increasingly likely for Northern Ireland, Best was inches away from signing with Middlesbrough. He had appeared in Teesside in a testimonial for San Jose teammate and former Middlesbrough stalwart Jim Platt, against derby rivals Sunderland. Best was so on it that day that McMurdo immediately got a call from Middlesbrough boss Bobby Murdoch with another, eye-wateringly highball offer. So, Best got on a flight from San Jose to Teesside via London.

Sadly, Best's flight to London was forced to kill time in the air because of a snowstorm. He started drinking during that delay, then left the airport in London when he arrived and went on a bender. Again, he kissed goodbye to being the UK's highest-paid player, and to any hope of a recall into Northern Ireland's 1982 World Cup side.

However, despite the romantic speculation, McMurdo is suspicious of Best's chances of making that World Cup squad regardless of the form he was in, because his profile wouldn't have worked with manager Billy Bingham's hardworking team of battlers.

Back in the US at San Jose, Best was reacquainted with his former teammate Kidd. Kidd was on his own retirement tour of the NASL after a successful career in England with United, Arsenal, Man City, Everton and the Bolton Wanderers. He started in Atlanta before moving on to the Fort Lauderdale Strikers for a couple of seasons as he prepared for what would be a long and prosperous coaching career.

Kidd remembers catching up with Best while his Strikers were in San Jose. They shared a meal at an upmarket beachside restaurant with Strikers' owner Joe Robbie, who also owned the NFL's Miami Dolphins. There Kidd and Robbie, the former lawyer, politician and tobacco lobbyist, played darts with Best and reminisced.

"George never touched a drop. I have never seen George Best drunk," remembers Kidd, who must be pleased he was reacquainted with his friend during a sober period in his life.

Best played in hundreds of testimonials, friendlies and exhibition games in the years while he was still somewhere near his peak, and sometimes a thrilling goal would bring his name back to the surface of boardrooms across Britain. If the old magic was back, then there were more than a couple of clubs willing to give him a shot at Football League redemption.

But Best, his family and entourage were nervous about playing in Britain with its media and temptations. His relationship with wife Angie was fluid to say the least, even after their first child Calum was born early in 1981. Angie told the media, in a frank and honest view of Best's character:

"We can't live together and we can't live apart. I still feel he's my little George. He'll have a string of girls, of course, but they won't be around a lot unless he's serious about them. I want to be friends with all of George's girlfriends, and he'll have to make it clear to them that I'm his pal."

Her instincts were right. By the early 80s, Best was also seeing actress and model Mary Stavin, living with her in the Barbican in London.

In 1982, Best commenced the first of many journeys to Hong Kong as a play toy for the nouveau riche. In November, he played a game for the Hong Kong Rangers. Apparently, Best's name on the marquee had seen a fourfold increase in crowds, but, according to Andrew Dettre, "after a pathetic display ... he had to be substituted [and then] came a quick exit."

But Bill McMurdo has more fond memories of Hong Kong as an epicentre for weird encounters:

"One time in Hong Kong, we played with South China. The woman who owned it was called Veronica Choo, and she met us at the airport in a pink Rolls-Royce. So, we are sitting there and she asks George, 'Anything you need or want to ask me?' He says, 'Well, I was a little bit taken aback with a pink Rolls-Royce.' She laughed. She turned up the following day with a white Rolls-Royce; she said, 'I took on board yesterday what you said, George.' Seven days, seven different Rolls-Royces. She was fucking minted. Absolutely minted."

On another occasion in Hong Kong, McMurdo recalls Best's celebrity power being laid bare:

"We had just arrived in Hong Kong. I was blocking all of the calls sitting there.

UN-UNITED (1975-1982)

The phone goes so I picked up the phone—and we had about 100 calls before this one—and this guy with a Liverpool accent says, 'George, please.' 'Can you say who's calling?' I asked. 'It is a personal call' the voice answered. 'You need to give me a name.' 'I'm not giving you a name,' he insisted. So finally, I said, 'Well if you don't give me a name, you're not going to get fucking put through, so please yourself.' 'He knows me. Tell him it's Richard Starkey,' was the man's begrudging response. I didn't know who it was. I said, 'Hold on a minute.' I said, 'George, I've got this guy on the phone for you, he said you know him, he's called Richard Starkey.' He went, 'Fuck, Bill, that's Ringo!'" recalls McMurdo fondly, despite having to then share an awkward dinner that night with the subject of his confusion.

Ringo Starr and his wife, Barbara, were on their way back from Australia and wanted to catch up with Best for dinner. Needless to say, Ringo was unimpressed by McMurdo's grasp of pop culture.

With his UK club career largely finished, and the next phase of his itinerant playing career bearing fruit, Best's financial prospects were looking bright. He was a bankable product—his early crowds for both Fulham and Hibernian were excellent, and he had a brand that was admired in most corners of the globe.

But Best was also trying to outrun his past mistakes, and 1982–83 was a period where everything seemed to collapse on him. Firstly, he was declared bankrupt and summoned to Bankruptcy Court over a tax bill from his time with Fulham. Nearly £18,000 was owed to Inland Revenue. In court, Best's overall debts to all parties were exposed as being over £100,000. To prevent bankruptcy, Best offered to pay the taxman £10,000 and the rest in six months, but the government wasn't buying.

The Assistant Official Receiver, Mr John Booth, adjourned the payback proceedings until July 26, 1983. His withering assessment of Best was a succinct summary of his adult decision-making:

"You receive the acclaim of society for your art and sport, but when it came to contributing to society for tax ... you failed to do so. All your income has been spent on living, gambling, drinking and expensive cars."

Best's only valuable investment—indeed it was listed as his only asset (according to reports on proceedings published by Reuters)—was his reported $25,000 investment in a Scottish company: McMurdo's 'George Best Management'. In fact, personal bankruptcy was a problem but not a catastrophe for Best. He was living in America during much of that time and had until recently been paid there. And his apartment in the Barbican, where both McMurdo and Best lived with Mary Stavin, was also owned by George Best Management. According to McMurdo, it was their Scottish company that collected Best's cheques.

The bankruptcy proceedings were an open wound that Best had lived with since his Fulham days, and they were only resolved once Best found a good lawyer and after the people of Belfast came to the aid of their favourite son and filled Windsor Park for a Best testimonial match in 1988. The George Best XI won 7-6, featuring Paul Breitner and Ruud Krol, overcoming an 'International XI' that included Ossie Ardiles, Trevor Francis and Johan Neeskens. Sir Matt Busby and old friend Michael Parkinson were there to support him.

According to McIlvanney:

"With the help of £72,000 raised by a testimonial match and dinner in Belfast, Best was able at last to lift a shadow that had darkened his spirits for more than a decade. ('The people of Belfast have sorted my whole life out,' he says emotionally.)"

But back in March 1983, Best needed to move on to his next gig—Third-Division side Bournemouth. This wasn't the ideal move for him as it involved a League commitment in the UK where his spotlight was the brightest. But Bournemouth's offer came with a tantalising kicker—they expected very little of him.

At Bournemouth, he wasn't really expected to train or fully integrate into the team, and in *Blessed*, Best described it like a marriage of convenience.

"I didn't have to train much, just show up, do a few tricks, earn the club some money and everyone was happy. Everyone understood each other. Most of those clubs got their money back from my first game so that it almost didn't matter if no one showed up for the second one."

Best had other offers he could consider but settled on Bournemouth. He claimed in *Blessed* that

'Big Ron' Atkinson's Manchester United was the first to reach out, but Best felt he wasn't ready for a challenge like United. He did not want to become a sideshow at the club he loved, and although it ended sourly, Best always had the memories of '68 and what he achieved with that part of his life. He did not want to sour those times with a footnote.

Other clubs he liked to flirt with, but he could never let Manchester United see his decline first-hand. He loved the club too much to let it down.

So, Best headed to the south coast to boost crowds and train when he wanted to. And maybe to sprinkle a bit of Best magic on the lower leagues.

A popular Bournemouth blog site, Cherry Chimes, has slightly different recollections on Best's time on the south coast:

"At 36 and in the grip of alcoholism, Best was a shadow of the player who had put fear into the hearts of defences across Europe in the 1960s, but his fading skills and box-office appeal were enough to briefly bring the crowds back to Dean Court."

In Best's debut against Newport, he doubled the average gate and drew 9,121. Bournemouth had unofficially agreed to only play him in home games in contravention of League rules. For away games, manager Don Megson would fabricate reasons not to pick him, often using his well-known, dodgy right knee as an excuse. But soon enough,

Megson would have to contrive the same excuse for different reasons entirely.

Before Easter in 1983, Best's much beloved landlady and Mancunian mother figure, Mary Fullaway, died. Her passing reopened the wound of his mother Anne's death in 1978 due to alcoholism. Best was given a leave of absence from 'the Cherries' to mourn Fullaway, and he didn't make it back for their home game against Leyton Orient. It kickstarted a trend of absences, with Bournemouth adding a new message to their ensemble of gate signs:

'GEORGE BEST WILL NOT BE PLAYING TODAY'

Bournemouth management would go looking for Best and find themselves driving around pubs in South London hoping to return their golden goose. But in between his dalliances with alcohol while he was there, Bournemouth actually helped Best reconnect to the aspects of football he was missing in exhibition games: being part of a team, training as a squad and general shenanigans in the dressing rooms. While he wasn't expected to train, when he was present, he was there because he enjoyed doing it.

Best never had a problem with training. He loved it. But it was the obligation clashing with his off-field choices that was the problem.

Harry Redknapp was at the start of his coaching journey with Bournemouth at the time. He recalls a jovial Best, in between his excursions to London's pubs.

"George was great," recalled Redknapp for Cherry Chimes:

"He came to training, he was just fantastic. I still don't think I've seen a better player in this country. He was one of the lads. Came in, trained every day. The lads couldn't believe they had got him here to play. I think he absolutely loved it here. George was enjoying his life, still playing."

However, journalists were not in the habit of cutting Best any slack. At that time, Bournemouth weren't the Premier League (or thereabouts) side that they are today, and Fairfax writer Peter Smark, based in London at the time, wrote:

"Bournemouth is not a soccer hotbed. It is where genteel middle classes go to retire. They gave George a sympathetic ovation. 'Sad to be cynical,' wrote one sportswriter who witnessed the occasion. 'But you suspected that the town of twilight people had recognised a kindred spirit.'"

Best was damned either way. Outside of his debut—where he likely received a share of the gate—Best was being paid next to nothing to appear for Bournemouth. There was a running commentary that he was the lowest paid pro in "the 96", earning only £35 a week.

The media oscillated between muckraking and hoping he would disappear when he was honest about his troubles. They didn't want to treat his problems seriously and treated them like a distraction from the character of Best that fed the tabloid sales machine.

Many things were unravelling in early 1983 for Best. Bournemouth had been a bust, and in May Angie left Best for good and moved back to LA with their son Calum, to make it as an actress. Bournemouth had also moved on. Best couldn't curtail his drinking and had gone AWOL one too many times.

With his life falling apart, he made a surprising decision. He would *not* let the grief consume him via drink.

While Best was a diagnosed and self-confessed alcoholic, he was able to choose sobriety at various times of his life. He had an element of control over his addiction that when he was near rock bottom and knew he needed to change course, he could choose a path without alcohol.

So, Best turned to sobriety in 1983. As a drinker, he knew when he had pushed his limits and could embrace periods of sobriety to try and rebuild damage he had done to relationships (and his career). He told writer Bill Mellor:

"Now I stick to tea … at last, at 36, I feel I've grown up … This year I have learned more and changed more than any other year in my life."

Mellor, in true Fleet Street fashion, had his doubts, responding in print:

"Readers could be forgiven for treating these statements with some scepticism," and labelled the claim a media stunt.

But this time it wasn't. Best was truly desperate to get his life back on track. There were often times in his life when he sought help. Bill McMurdo confirms this, citing multiple periods where Best didn't touch a drop. He had the ability to switch off the addiction in these moments of clarity and despair, but sadly for Best, they didn't last.

"We had a flat in London [and we] stayed there for a couple of years and he would say he was going to stop drinking on the Wednesday, and I said, 'That's great.' When he was drinking solidly, he would drink solidly for three or four months just day or night, he wouldn't shave or whatever. On the Wednesday, he would get up in the morning and have a shower and have a shave and he would look like a million dollars, who else could do that? Who else could drink for three months, drink themselves into oblivion and then get up and have a shower and then look like fucking Sean Connery? It was just unbelievable."

Shortly before arriving in Australia, Best's beloved Manchester United won the FA Cup, and Best joined his old teammates Denis Law and Bobby Charlton in the coverage. Best was spritely, in great humour and appeared in his element.

However, the wreckage of his life weighed on his shoulders. Hugh McIlvanney interviewed Best in 1992 about his alcoholism, and wrote:

"He has convinced himself that the best compromise he can manage in his efforts to cope with his drink problem is an attempt to shorten the binges and lengthen the periods when the craving is under control."

Australia in 1983 was certainly one of those *lengthened periods*.

"I'd be sitting in AA meetings longing for them to end, so I could get to a bar," he said. "When I was supposed to be swallowing those tablets that make you allergic to alcohol–I was married to Angela, the mother of my son, at the time–I was sometimes hiding them behind my teeth and getting rid of them later. And even when I had the implants, I was saying to myself, 'When the effect of these pellets wears off, I'll have a good drink.' So those therapies didn't have much chance of working."

Best was taking Antabuse tablets orally before the Australian trip. But just when he started trying the Antabuse as an implant isn't clear. It's possible that just before arriving in Australia, he had the tablets surgically implanted in his stomach. Best played in Norway on May 17 in a friendly against Norwich City, so the timing is possible.

Henk Mollee, who sat on the board at the Brisbane Lions in 1983, recalls McMurdo talking about the surgery with him so there is every chance the surgery occurred just before his Australian tour.

McMurdo remembers a night "out" with Best shortly after the surgery, and after they had hopped a flight to Vancouver. He remembers that experience incredulously:

"We had just arrived [in Vancouver] and there were two beds in the one room, he was in one bed and I was in the other bed watching some TV. I heard this 'ping'. I thought, 'What the fuck's that?' He started laughing. I said, 'What are you laughing at?' ... He had opened his wound to take his fucking tablets out and pinged them in the fucking bin. He said, 'That means I can have a drink tonight.' He said that the stitches burst, and he took them out, but he was pinging them in this fucking bin. Fortunately, he never had a drink the whole time we were there the two weeks, but he could have done. He had that [surgery] done another time too. I think he had that done two or three times."

As Best tried to put the pieces of his life together in mid-1983, having sworn off alcohol, an offer came in for him to join the Brisbane Lions. He had played 50 or so times in the last 12 months for Bournemouth but mostly in friendlies and exhibition games. So, he had some kind of fitness base, certainly one he felt he could work with.

Best also had marvellous memories of Australia. In 1967, he ran rings around national and state rep sides, and still had an impression of Australia as a warm (both of heart and temperature) and welcoming place. Australia probably seemed the perfect place to go to feel the sun again after driving away so many clouds.

But he knew that the media would be on top of him the moment he arrived, reminding him constantly of his past. Mary Stavin wouldn't be joining him. She was off in South America promoting the Bond movie *Octopussy* where she was cast as one of seventeen 'Octopussy girls'. So, there would be multiple temptations to disturb his new, cloistered lifestyle.

Despite the hope and positivity going into his Australian tour, there would also be another ghost of his past he couldn't avoid: Tommy Docherty. For the non-confrontational Best, being forced onto pitches and TV sets with Docherty would feel like being fed to lions. Unlike Androcles, there were no wounded animals he could turn to for help. Facing a foreign tabloid media, Best needed friends—people who could vouch for him.

Instead, there was only Docherty, who thought—or at least expressed to the media—that Best had poisoned the well for him in 1974. Docherty used every trick up his sleeve to turn the football community, and the media, against Best.

Best blamed Docherty for his exit from United and blamed him entirely for their relegation in 1974. And their frostiness grew over the years. On a local Mancunian phone-in radio programme in 1981 when Docherty first accepted a coaching role in Australia (with Sydney Olympic), Best wished Docherty well before asking, on air, "Tell me Doc… is it true that you're going to coach in Australia because that's where the convicts go?"

After a moment of hesitation, taking in the slight, Docherty replied "You'd like Australia too, George, some fo the Aussies drink nearly as much as you!"

Perhaps the most bizarre subplot to the 1983 tour of Australia is Best's description of it in *Blessed*. Either the years had been unkind to Best's memory, or, for brevity in the book, he boiled down every element of the tour into one quick grab that was approximate to the truth:

"I flew off on a tour in the Far East with Bill McMurdo, playing for a couple of teams in Hong Kong and then for the Brisbane Lions in Australia. A guy named Ed Marconi owned them and we had some pretty good attendance in the three games I had agreed to play for them. So, he asked me to play one final match, a special game he was trying to organise against their biggest rivals—I can't remember what they were called. It wasn't part of my deal, so he said, 'Tell you what, George. It's bound to be a big gate, so I'll split the attendance money with you.' The Lions game turned out to be my last club appearance."

There is no Ed Marconi. Best signed on for three games with the Brisbane Lions, and signed on for a bonus game *against* Marconi where he received a share of the gate.

And while it is true that the Lions were Best's National League side, after Brisbane he played in Adelaide, then a State League game in Perth, before returning to Sydney for an exhibition game. He got part of the story right. And Ed Marconi does sound like a very Australian football manager's name.

Best's printed memory of the trip is indicative of the media commentary around his arrival in 1983, and stories of his visit that are shared today among fans, players and administrators. The details around his tour have become myth and legend but, ultimately, what he brought to Australia was a little different to what everyone was expecting.

Fed to the Lions (1983)

It was nearly 16 years to the day that Best arrived in Brisbane in 1983 after his 1967 visit. He was a very different player to the one that buried the Queensland state side 7–0 at the Brisbane Exhibition Ground in front of 32,000 fans. As outlined earlier in the book, Best scored twice that day.

Now, Best was 37, bearded, bankrupt and trying to turn over a new leaf.

After he landed in Brisbane, he told local reporters:

"I'm as fit as one can be at 37. Of course, I don't compare for pace with the player I was 10 years ago. But skill—that improves with age."

Skill was what the Lions desperately needed. In 1983, they were a poor team with workman-like players. Their mediocre attendances were also in need of star billing. And the Lions were willing to pay it—$50,000, to be precise, for three games and a number of coaching and speaking engagements.

It was a major gamble for the Lions, especially considering how much $50,000 could get them in 1983. Socceroo striker John Kosmina had cost Sydney City $45,000 for his entire contract in 1981.

But the Lions were in the import game and had been for years. Bob Latchford (1981) and Alan Sunderland (1982) had both come from the English League and scored buckets of goals. They turned a workman-like squad into winners on the pitch. However, while neither Latchford nor Sunderland transformed their crowd figures, Best had a pulling power that was far greater than your standard League Golden Boot or FA Cup winner.

Former club director Henk Mollee describes the Brisbane ethos at the time:

"Lions have always been a club that's been forward looking, forward striving. We've always tried to please the public and the supporters. This is what it was for. It was to give the club a boost, which it did, because our name was there for a while. We tried to up our following in the National League and this is how we did it."

The Brisbane Lions trace their origins to Dutch migrants to Queensland, and they were founded in 1957 as the Hollandia Inala Soccer Club. Henk Mollee's connection to the club goes so far back that he was the club's inaugural first-team goalkeeper.

In 1975, as a mainstay in the Queensland Leagues, Hollandia adopted the Brisbane Lions name as leagues across the country discouraged the use of ethnic-oriented team names. The Lions were founding members of the National Soccer League in 1977 along with cross-town rivals Brisbane City.

The Brisbane Lions of today are known as the Queensland Lions in the top division of football in Queensland, but they also played a part in the formation of the Brisbane Roar A-League club. The Roar's matching orange jerseys are a tribute to their Dutch origins.

Like many football clubs in Australia, their 'ethnic' origin story became less noticeable on the pitch (or in the stands) over time, but persisted in the surnames of board members, major sponsors and benefactors.

One such benefactor was businessman Hans Strik. He was central, along with Mollee, in doing the deal for Best.

Bill McMurdo recalls that the deal was first floated to Best by former Lions manager Joe Gilroy, and then driven over the line by Dutch-born promoter and businessman Strik. Gilroy was manager of the Lions in 1981 and 1982, and just happened to be in the right place at the right time:

"What happened was we were flying to LA from Glasgow, [Best] and I. We met a guy who used to play for Brisbane Lions, a Scotsman called Joe Gilroy, he was also a coach. We got talking on the plane. He said, 'Would you come to Australia?' We said, 'If the terms were right.' So, I gave him my number. A guy called Hans Strik got in touch with us on behalf of Joe Gilroy.

"I said, 'Look, if you can put this whole thing together and it's worthwhile financially and all the rest of it, then we would love the opportunity to do it but it has got to be a package, we need hotels and flights and cash and the whole bit.' After about two or three weeks of putting it all together, we had Malaysian Airlines sponsor us first class all the way to Australia and back. On the way back in Kuala Lumpur, we did a thing for the Malaysian FA where we did coaching schools."

Gilroy was replaced after 1982 by Dutchman Simon Kistemaker, but the seed he had planted germinated into a full package deal with flights and accommodation for the 1983 season.

After agreeing to the deal, McMurdo started exploring other business and media opportunities for Best. An easy win was the *Parkinson* show, filmed in Sydney at the time by Best's good personal friend, Michael Parkinson. It was an Australian version of his successful British format and aired on Channel 10. Other TV and radio programs were also booked, as well as autograph signings in flagship shops like Benetton.

Henk Mollee remembers the signing a little differently. Mollee had met with Best on something of a scouting trip to the UK a couple of years before 1983. According to

FED TO THE LIONS (1983)

Mollee, Best wasn't in great physical shape when they met, but he was open to the idea.

Perhaps Mollee planted a seed that germinated with Joe Gilroy's chance meeting, but what is known for certain is that Best was in a lot better shape when he landed in 1983 than when he first met with the Lions director.

Before Best joined, new Lions manager Simon Kistemaker had been trying to build a new-look squad. They'd signed Airdrie midfielder Jim McDonagh on a $4,000 deal and just missed out on Socceroo John Yzendoorn (who opted for South Melbourne instead). Kistemaker was an import himself and had experience in the Eredivisie in the Netherlands. He was more a 'total football' man than the dour football style the Lions had previously been known for.

Other recent imports—Billy Williamson, Mark Atmore and Boudewijn de Geer—were moved on to make way for Best. de Geer was a big ticket signing from the Netherlands in early 1983 but had been a total disaster. They cut him loose after a handful of games.

"He was unfit and wilted in the hot Queensland sun" was the club's withering assessment provided to Soccer Action.

Despite the wheeling and dealing, the Lions season started poorly. In mid-May they were smashed by cross-city rivals, Brisbane City, 4-0. In the aftermath of the game, there were reports in the media that former Lions player Jim Hermiston, who was then with City, threw a bucket of water over Lions boss Simon Kistemaker. Kistemaker became "enraged" by the act and had to be held back by his players.

Lions goalkeeper on that day, Nigel Lownds, didn't see that incident, and doubts that 'Gentleman Jim'—who went on to have an illustrious career in the Queensland Police Force—would stoop to that. But if he did, something must have seriously put him over the edge.

"I didn't like Simon Kistemaker. I didn't like his style of coaching," Lownds conceded, reflecting today on the Kistemaker era. "He was an arrogant man. I could imagine me throwing a bottle of water on him."

Best's imminent arrival was an opportunity for the Lions to kick-start their faltering season. The timing was perfect for both club and player.

He arrived in Sydney's Mascot Airport on 28 June and was immediately swamped by reporters. A press conference awaited him in a private room at the airport, and Best sipped tea and told the baying Australian press that he was "on the wagon" and he "hadn't touched the bottle in six months". While this claim wasn't *technically* correct, he knew how to work the media well enough to get his point across.

Sadly, much of his statement fell on deaf ears. More than one report of the press conference included inane remarks about not detecting a "whiff of booze" on him.

He was barely through Australian Customs at Mascot before the press was turning on him. In the room full of microphones and regular press ('soccer media' back then were a handful of people), it was clear that 'Best the drunk' had preceded him off the plane, and Best the footballer, or Best the human being needn't have bothered alighting.

"I don't have a drinking problem. I'm an alcoholic ... there's a difference," he told the Sydney media who had their noses at the ready. Best was staring into the abyss once more.

Most reporters were disappointed by the Best sitting before them. He was not what they were expecting. He looked lean and healthy, almost sanguine. *The Age* was one of the few publications to read the room correctly, reporting that "A sleek-looking athlete with black shiny hair, neatly clipped beard, lively face and dancing eyes bounced ahead of his manager and soccer officials into the VIP interview room at Mascot Airport."

Some were incredulous about this sober iteration of Best. The *Sydney Morning Herald*'s rugby league writer, Gary Lester, seemed put out that Best hadn't downed a bottle of whiskey:

"On arrival, Best even had the hide to sip tea ... reformed? Nothing has changed in soccer."

There was definitely more to that press conference than Best realised at the time. Indeed, the media expectations had been spelt out for them. An agent provocateur working with the media had been painting a specific picture of Best for weeks.

This was the first of many penitences Best would be asked to endure. The man who had been speaking to the media, and who was also awaiting Best in that VIP room, was the man who sacked him at United, Tommy Docherty.

Best knew that Docherty was living and coaching in Australia at Sydney Olympic, who would be the Lions first opponents in 1983. Before they left London for Australia, McMurdo told AAP:

"George and Tommy have crossed swords many times before. They have a special love-hate relationship which has lasted many years, but it's one tinged with mutual respect."

That was an optimistic take. Best despised Docherty. He blamed him for his divorce from United, and he grew to resent Docherty further when implicating Best in United's relegation in 1974.

Biographer Duncan Hamilton wrote:

"His forgiveness didn't stretch as far as Tommy Docherty. In the months immediately following his departure, he pretended to be ambivalent about United because he didn't want to give Docherty the satisfaction of knowing how much it meant to him. In the years that followed it, his antagonism toward Docherty hardened. He held him—and no one else—responsible for his exit."

It came as a horrible shock to Best to find Docherty, and his good friend Michael Parkinson, sitting in the VIP room alongside the Lions powerbroker, Hans Strik. When he entered the room, Docherty hugged Best like they were old friends.

Beforehand at the press conference, Strik boldly announced that Best would draw 4,000 extra fans to each game.

"We're paying him the highest ever fee offered by Australian soccer, but it's worth it."

Strik himself is a curious character, and exactly the sort of independently wealthy businessman who was commonly found in the boardrooms and back rooms at NSL clubs. He was a used car salesman, property developer, entrepreneur and long-time supporter of (now disgraced) Queensland Premier, Sir Joh Bjelke-Petersen. In 2003, Strik tried to sell two paintings done by Sir Joh and his wife, Lady Flo, to help the couple cover legal costs. He'd bought the paintings in 1978 for $50,000. His asking price in 2003 was $1,000,000 for the pair (he planned to give Sir Joh half of that). Hans Strik clearly had a keen eye for value.

Indeed, at the time Best's signing was announced, Strik named his next two targets: Johan Cruyff and Kevin Keegan. While Keegan fans didn't need to wait long to see him in the NSL - he played 2 games for Blacktown City in 1985 - "Total Football" never came to Redlands; outside of Simon Kistemaker's particular incarnation of it.

After the press conference, McMurdo remembers football reporter David Jack (the second), who had emigrated to Sydney from Manchester over a decade earlier, approaching him and Best. Jack had known Best for years during his days on the Manchester beat.

"He said, 'I'm very surprised to see you cuddling Tommy Doherty.' George said, 'Ahh, you know, like it's expats abroad.' 'You see, George,' Jack replied, 'he fucking slaughtered you before you came here in all the papers, for wasting money and leaving England, and all sorts. The Lions are spending money when they should be bringing through youth players and all this nonsense, right?' So, he showed us all the cuttings and we knew it had been very scary. They said 'drunkard', 'alcoholic', all these things."

To really drive the lion's tooth into Best's heart, Docherty was also booked to appear with him on Channel 7's *Sportscene* before his debut against Olympic, alongside host David Fordham.

After the shock of encountering his nemesis on his arrival, Best was taken to a private interview with Channel 10 and established football journalist, Tommy Anderson. This was the first of many interviews where Best would be asked about his fall from grace.

"Have you got any regrets, you know, if you'd had more discipline, for instance, that you could have really reached the top?"

"Not really. I was at the top for 12 good years," replied the Ballon d'Or and European Cup winner.

After Sydney, Best and McMurdo then boarded a flight to Brisbane to join his new teammates. When he first arrived at training, there was another expat in the squad there to greet him who had some prior experience with Best.

Mike Mulvey was a Mancunian kid who went through United's Academy before emigrating to Australia in late 1982. He went on to have a successful career in management in the A-League with Gold Coast United (as caretaker), then the Brisbane Roar before taking over the Central Coast Mariners. With the Mariners, he had the extremely rare distinction of managing Usain Bolt in his brief stint with the club.

When Mulvey was growing up a United fan, Best was the cornerstone of the United sides he adored.

"I do remember going to Old Trafford, my dad had a season ticket … and he used to give a packet of Woodbines to the guy who would let me go through the gate. I would pay to go into the standing area and then [they would] send me up into the seats when I was 7, 8, 9 and [I] used to sit on my dad's lap and watch the game. George Best, Bobby Charlton, Denis Law … we were spoiled because you had these three geniuses you could see every week. I was brought up on a diet of that and it was obviously special when he came and played in Brisbane in the early 1980s," Mulvey recalls fondly.

He was also one of many thousands who took the opportunity to 'pop in' to Best's luxury, custom-built house in Bramhall, south of Manchester. When it was built in 1969, it became a popular tourist attraction for fans, well-wishers and the occasional stalker. Best had to live elsewhere at times to avoid the attention. He even had a moat installed on the property, but that didn't deter visitors.

"I remember on one Sunday, my dad said, 'Come on, let's go and have a look at George's house.' There were so many cars there, people were just driving by to see him and his house. Obviously, he wasn't there at that time but if I look back now, I keep thinking how much pressure must the guy have been under. How relentless the people must have been in pursuit of him."

Over a decade later, they were teammates, and Best had just arrived in Mulvey's dressing room. Best integrated quickly. On the training pitch, he still had something resembling 'it', while in the rooms he had a lot of 'it' too, which was his ability to captivate his younger teammates with stories about his after-hours activities.

Goalkeeper Nigel Lownds, Macclesfield-born and who had been on the books of Macclesfield Town, Bury and Manchester City as a youngster, especially enjoyed his time seated beside Best in the training rooms.

Lownds, like Mulvey, has a very familiar British ex-pat NSL story arc. A youth prospect in North West England, he was looked at by some famous clubs before a career in the lower leagues beckoned. But the lure of making a career out of football while some sun shone on his back was too great. In fact, Lownds was almost on a plane to Vancouver to join the Whitecaps before the Brisbane offer came "out of the blue".

"My wife and I preferred to come to Australia than go to Canada," Lownds recalls, invoking Brisbane's famously anti-Lancashire weather.

Lownds was present for the Bob Latchford and Alan Sunderland Brisbane era, and he remembers Best today as a generally affable and humble man. He and Best got along famously.

"Goalkeepers are a bit extroverted, you know."

Best sat beside Lownds before and after training because, simply, Lownds often had a free seat next to him when Best first walked into training. Lownds' Lancashire accent might have also struck a familiar chord with Best.

Lownds recalls that Best's dry wit sometimes went over his head, but more importantly, Best's banter was elite—and there was a lot to go around with all of Best's collected anecdotes. To outsiders and club officials, Lownds and Best seemed to immediately bond over a common interest in Best's catalogue of sexual conquests.

"You know what lads are like in the dressing room," is Lownds' recollection of it. And seated beside a man often portrayed as an arch-Lothario, it's only natural that some clarification would be sought.

"I told him that I used to dream of Marjorie Wallace, and he said, 'Yeah, so did I.' But I was talking about a magazine and he was talking about the real thing," Lownds recalls, invoking Best's well-reported, brief 1973 fling with the former Miss World, which ended bizarrely in Best being arrested (and later exonerated) for stealing some of her personal items.

Lownds also remembers Best as a man who was 'apart' from his teammates. While he was approachable and charming in his own way, he wasn't quite one of the lads. And there wasn't any real socialising happening with teammates off the pitch.

"He was very personable, but he was happy to get away at the end of the day."

At the time, Lownds put this down to him still drinking—or being haunted by it. While Lownds never saw Best drink, there were moments that prompted him to wonder.

When asked about Best's noted 1983 sobriety, Lownds replied, "I'm not so sure about that."

While he doesn't recall any socialising with Best, Mike Mulvey remembers him hosting a lunch for teammates at the Crest Hotel where he was staying. And while it wasn't a rager, it was an olive branch from Best to his teammates.

Mulvey wasn't privy to Best's after-hours work during his stint and, frankly, there wasn't much to be privy to. Best went to bed at nine to read or do the crossword—which he could reportedly finish in a couple of minutes.

Players, opponents, the media and hangers-on at the club were all a bit disappointed to find Best the first to leave the dressing room.

The closest thing Best had to a 'night out' in Brisbane were some dinners with actor Kenneth Branagh, who was also in town. On his days off, McMurdo and Best hit the Gold Coast to work on their tans and they also took some time off to check out the Great Barrier Reef.

McMurdo still laughs today about 'the saint inside the sinner' side of Best.

"When George wasn't drinking, he was the most boring fucking man in life. He would stay in at 10 o'clock at night having a cup of tea and then bed."

Best, the famous pants man, also left that part of his life in England. His relationship status was fairly "complicated", but Mary Stavin was his long-time partner, and he was still—on some level—grieving the end of his marriage to Angie. McMurdo confirms that Best "never looked at a woman in Australia at all, which was unlike him."

Like Lownds, Mulvey remembers Best being quiet, but respected his professionalism when it came to training.

"He was still a very charismatic quiet character, and he was one of the lads. He got in, he mucked in. I had Usain Bolt... at the Mariners and I would say it was very similar, Usain came in and he was very unassuming, he turned up and did his work."

And while Usain Bolt's pre-season matches for the Central Coast Mariners didn't quite work out—or worked about as well as everyone anticipated—hopes were a lot higher for Best.

On the training pitch, Best still had a lot of his old tricks. Mulvey remembers Best in his pomp at training.

"At training, he was nutmegging people for fun. As I have moved into the coaching arena, you understand about keeping possession and when and where to do things. One of the things about nutmegging someone is it's okay to do it as long as you keep possession. A lot of people do it and they can't keep possession after it. It looks good, but they've lost the ball. George Best would keep the ball. It used to be said from people in England [that] there are two balls on the pitch, give one to George and everyone else can play with the other one."

McMurdo concurs.

"George is a footballer that enjoyed everything about football. He enjoyed the dressing room and the comradery and whole buildup. That's what kept him going. He enjoyed all that and the thing is he would get totally involved in that. He wouldn't just turn up. They would be surprised by how thorough he was, the whole training and that, but that is just how he was. Old habits die hard, he was always a good trainer."

When he was present at training, Best was an elite performer, and when he was sober, he maintained a genuinely high fitness base. He had built up an engine from his early days fanatically training with United that he carried into the 'exhibition phase' of his career. Clubs who expected a washed-up husk of a trainer were often surprised that he was, mostly, willing and able to do the work on the track.

However, before Best could show his new employer what he was capable of on match day, he had to endure a morning interview with journalist David Fordham and his nemesis Tommy Docherty. He was an old hand at appeasing the press and used

FED TO THE LIONS (1983)

humour to defuse awkward situations, so he got on the front foot by opening with, "You're very fortunate I'm usually on the way home at this time of morning."

That seemed to embolden Fordham to put one on the tee for Docherty.

FORDHAM: "Tom, you were a bit concerned that George may not have arrived here this morning."

DOCHERTY: "He's cost me $200 this week already. He's turned up twice. I'm getting a bit worried now."

It was a joke Docherty had obviously worked on and rehearsed, as he used it again in another interview after the Olympic game in Brisbane.

Soon, Fordham fed Docherty another line.

FORDHAM (smirking like a Cheshire Cat): You also had a brief dealing with George, didn't you, in the early 70s?

DOCHERTY: Yeah, in '73 George came, he did marvellous for us actually, then he did the Martin Bormann touch again and buzzed off for a holiday. You look at all these clips about him and this and that but the only people I saw really drunk was the defenders that he roasted alive on the field ... He's a genius.

It was a heavily weighted backhander.

Firstly, Best had predated Docherty at United by a decade and so he hadn't 'come down' anywhere. As the camera panned to Best for the Martin Bormann comment (Bormann was Deputy Fuhrer to Hitler and tried to escape Berlin after Hitler's suicide in 1945), all Best could do was nervously wince. But inside, he was fuming.

At the break, a furious Best approached McMurdo and said, "I'm going to have him."

"I don't even think we knew he was going to be there until we actually got there," McMurdo recalls. "Then when we got there, it just rekindled everything again, so George just had a go at him."

Bill McMurdo witnessed the whole thing.

"George got totally unruly. He fucking says, 'You're sitting here telling everybody how good it is for me to be here. You never said that two weeks ago when you absolutely left me for dead,'" recalls McMurdo, with Best referring to the slander Docherty had aired before his arrival.

Afterwards, a contrite Docherty approached McMurdo.

"Tommy said to me after, 'I never meant to offend him.' I said, 'Tommy, look at what you said, right? They should save the money, etc. That's what's offended him. I think you're out of order for the fact that you slagged him publicly, told them how to spend their money and invest it in different ways. We come here [and now] you're cuddling the two of us like we're long-lost brothers.'"

"He said, 'Well, that's me.'"

Before the spat, and most certainly captured on air, Best put out a call to fans and the football Gods about his expectations with the Lions:

"I think, and hope at the end of the day that people remember what I did on the field, and that's the only thing that concerns me really."

After staring into the abyss and facing his old demons, Best was itching to fight back on the pitch. When his round 16 debut against Sydney Olympic came around at Brisbane's Perry Park, he was eager to show the Lions that he was worth the investment, and to get one last victory over Docherty.

In the lead-up, Olympic star Peter Katholos, in his regular 'Kat's Corner' feature in *Soccer Action* (who had arranged for a photo of Best reading a copy surrounded by blonde models), was recycling some of Docherty's old gags:

"Well, Sydney Olympic and I are due to play against George Best on Sunday. I hope he turns up ... I reckon that signing him as a guest player doesn't say much for our soccer. To George Best, I say welcome to Australia. I look forward to playing against you and having a drink with you after the game."

Katholos was being tone deaf to say the least. Here he was talking about a European Cup and Ballon d'Or winner who was battling a serious addiction, but he was unable to muster any respect. The copy had Docherty's fingerprints all over it.

But while Katholos wasn't brimming with enthusiasm, others were. Lions vice president, Paul Templeton, who had brokered the Bob Latchford deal in 1981, told the *Sydney Morning Herald* in the buildup:

"We thoroughly checked whether Best could still produce his old magic when we signed him. We should attract Queensland's best club crowd to Perry Park."

On the morning of the Olympic game, the mood was electric. TV, radio and newspaper journalists, fans and autograph hunters all descended on Perry Park's grandstands and its ample standing room on the hills. Program sellers wore shirts saying:

'GEORGE DOES IT BEST.'

But while the excitement was palpable, Best himself was feeling some pressure.

"You know, I'm not superman," he told TV reporters. "Everybody plays badly once in a while. But I just hope that my bad games are a little less than normal."

This was a rare expression of nerves from Best, and it hinted at how much he wanted (or needed) his Australian tour to go well. It also demonstrated real vulnerability. While Best often touted the "skill doesn't age" line in public, maybe he was realising that at 37, not all his old tricks were still there.

If he couldn't deliver at least a facsimile of the old Best, then his whole venture into exhibition football was at risk. And if there wasn't the stability of football in this life, then even greater problems awaited him.

So, eager to deliver, Best joined his teammates for his fever-pitched debut.

Before kick-off, Simon Kistemaker approached Mike Mulvey with inspiring words.

"I remember him saying to me, look this is your boyhood hero, go and play and enjoy it, this is something you will remember forever. He was right about that, but I didn't have a good game and I think I got pulled off just after half-time. I remember from the kick-off they kicked the ball to me and what do you do in a big game and your idol is on the field, you just give him the ball straight away. So, I gave him the ball and about four players converged on him, and he danced in and around them and passed the ball off to someone else and then said to me, 'Anytime you like, son.'"

Best, up against the coach that spurned him at his beloved Manchester United, found himself choked in the first half with the nerves he hinted at before the game. After the match, he elaborated for the media:

"I just wanted to pace myself and make sure I got through the 90 minutes as I only arrived a couple of days ago. I knew I was fit, but I'd never played with the Lions before and I wasn't sure what to expect. I also knew I'd have every eye watching me and while I'm used to that after all these years, it doesn't make it any easier those first couple of minutes."

The first half started poorly for Best and the Lions, and worsened when Best dislocated his finger and had to push it back into place on the pitch. The *Courier Mail* described his early role in the game as:

"[Keeping] Well clear of some robust midfield skirmishing, preferring to find space for himself in a deep-lying role on the left wing."

And his peripheral role became a problem after half an hour when his fullback opponent, Mike Coady, won the ball and drove forward while Best jogged beside him. Coady then put the ball into the channel for zinger-writer-cum-midfielder Peter Katholos to run onto the pass and score.

So far, Best had only stood out in the game for wearing a Malaysian Airlines logo on his jersey, while his teammates had KLM logos—the club's major sponsor—on theirs. Match reports had him only touching the ball 16 times in the first half before, finally, the real Best stood up and had a hand in the equaliser.

Five minutes before half-time, Best ghosted into a position at the top of the box and received the ball on his chest. He then turned his opponent, feinted one way and moved the other to leave his opponent sprawling. His flick-on then caught the hand of the defender, whose arms were flailing as though calling for a lifeboat. It was a golden opportunity at the top of the box that had Best's name written all over it.

But while everyone was watching Best ready himself for the kick, teammate Alan Niven snuck in like a cat burglar to steal a cherished memory for everyone. Niven slammed a quickly taken shot into the unexpectant wall, then got his own rebound and poked home the equaliser.

The Lions had scored, and this glimpse of Best magic inspired the crowd. In a wonderful piece of pun-work from *Soccer Action's* Margaret McDonald—who must have personally counted Best's touch and run stats herself—"Overheard on the terraces in the first half was, 'I thought he was the world's best' and 'He's not George Best. He's more like George "just adequate".' But in the second half, the Northern Irish soccer legend assumed a different identity, moving from just George Best to George 'absolutely marvellous'."

"Every time he touched the ball, he beat the tackler and flicked a superbly timed pass to one of his teammates, using an array of dazzling skills," reported the Courier Mail, who had also bought into the myth of Best.

A match report on Channel 10 agreed.

"Every time Best came onto the ball, the crowd roared with anticipation. He played the position to perfection. Always the opportunist, often unmarked when receiving and passing with amazing accuracy. The years have not dulled the Best magic."

Nigel Lownds, standing in goal at the other end of the pitch, remembers Best 'mesmerising' the opposition at times.

"We were a working side," Lownds believes. "And to have someone with that kind of skill who could hold onto the ball for such a period of time was just brilliant."

Best took all the corners, and during the second half while on corner duty, a fan raced to pitch side with an outstretched can of beer. But Best waved him away and sent another inch-perfect pass into the mixer.

Brisbane's winner came very late through the 88th-minute effort from Calvin Daunt. It ensured Best's debut was a winning one, and he had worked his way into the game, eventually winning over the crowd.

The official crowd figure was 5,000, but many who were there believe the number to be much higher, potentially beyond 10,000. Given that most 'official' NSL crowds are suspiciously listed as round numbers, we will never know precisely how many came out for Best.

Most importantly, Best had defeated Docherty's team. It was small comfort, but it was a wound landed on his former boss. After the final whistle, Docherty discussed the game with Channel 10's Tommy Anderson. He called the crowd "one of the biggest seen at Perry Park in a long while". Docherty repeated his "cost me $200" gag, and also his claim that Best "had been a genius in 1973".

But he stopped short of serious praise for Best's game against his Sydney Olympic.

"I thought he did quite well. I wouldn't sum him up any better than that. He's a good ambassador for the game. I thought he did well."

Docherty then checked his notes and moved on to other related topics. He called for "overseas players to be banned" for costing young Australian players game time. Presumably, his ban wouldn't apply to managers.

Olympic finished mid-table in 1983, and Docherty returned to England to go one more year in the Football League with Wolves, who were sliding rapidly down the pyramid. Docherty's tenure saw the side relegated from the Second Division, and he wouldn't get another job in England's top tiers.

Docherty passed away in 2020 at the age of 92, having led a full life in football. He was admired across the game and was a favourite interviewee for many because of his frankness and good humour. Sadly in 1983, George Best was often at the butt-end of that humour.

A Bit on the Side (1983)

Best's debut had been positive both on and off the pitch. The Lions saw attendance swell, and Best had done enough with the ball to suggest he had more to offer his new side.

He was pleased with his performance and had two games to look forward to the following week. There was a home clash with St George, and then an away clash in Sydney with Marconi. Originally, the Lions were not planning to include Best in away matches so as to keep all the gate-boosts for themselves, but Marconi were desperate to have Best on their pitch. So eager, in fact, that they offered the Lions a $7,500 transfer fee—of sorts—to let Best play for Marconi against them.

McMurdo believes the Lions were open to the offer, but that it didn't sit right with Best. After delicate negotiations, the Lions shared Marconi's counteroffer with McMurdo:

"The president from Marconi (whose name for the record was not Ed Marconi) is so convinced that George will bring many people to the game that he is prepared to pay a salary for George to play against Marconi."

That also didn't sit right with Best, but ultimately all parties landed on paying Best 75% of any gate receipts Marconi earned over $5,500. After pushing so hard for his appearance, only Marconi's team manager Fausto Ferrari paused to wonder, telling the *Sydney Morning Herald*:

"I only hope it doesn't backfire and that he does not help the Lions to beat us."

And there were other opportunities presenting themselves to McMurdo and his George Best Management company. In that same piece in the SMH, the Lions denied that Best had signed to play for one of Adelaide's NSL teams. And they were technically correct. Best wasn't about to appear in the NSL with a rival side, but he had signed to appear in an exhibition game for West Adelaide Hellas after his Lions commitments were complete.

It was also announced around this time that Best had signed on to appear for the pan-Yugoslav side Osborne Park Galeb in the Western Australian State League. Initially mooted as a two-game deal (Best only appeared once), the price tag was $8,500 per game, which was enough to send *Soccer Action* into apoplexy:

"So, while every NSL club struggles for financial survival, the former Manchester United and Northern Ireland star fits in and out of the local scene with a hefty fee to take back to the UK."

It was a common criticism of Best and Docherty had laid the groundwork for it. Money was—and still is—tight in Australian football, and noble visions of youth development and facility upgrades were at odds with what Best was offering.

The deal with Galeb was in place before Best arrived in Brisbane, but it was kept under wraps by the Best camp to let Brisbane get all the early positive PR. Now with the debut and the barrage of mixed press out of the way, Best and McMurdo started maximising the potential of the second half of the tour.

To prepare Western Australian Balkans for Best's arrival, Galeb sent a photographer from a Serbo-Croat language magazine to capture a day in the life of Best. The problem was that the photographer they sent was a Serb who spoke no English. McMurdo remembers the day fondly.

"This guy comes through the hotel with all these fucking cases and cameras, and shakes hands, doesn't speak a word of English right, and he is sat now at fucking breakfast. We go over to the lift, the lift is coming down. I turned around, the guy is fucking clicking me, and the camera is on me, George is looking at me laughing. I said, 'You're thinking what I'm thinking, aren't you? He thinks I'm you.' So, we get in the lift and he's fucking clicking away at me, I said, 'George, we've got to fucking tell him, if he goes back to the magazine after paying all of that money.' George said, 'I'm fucking loving this, right.' So, we kept it going for about an hour, but we tried to explain to him who was who, and we thought we got it eventually sorted out. But then we went to different suites, and he follows me. I open the door and he's clicking away. George is rolling about laughing. It was very funny."

Best's military routine while in Australia barely left him any free time outside of his scheduled trips across Queensland. This proved a blessing for someone trying to ignore the calling of his addiction. He ran free coaching sessions for the Lions—the five-day, 4BC-sponsored camp that Bob Latchford had hosted two years earlier. It drew hundreds of kids from other clubs' youth sides. He also made appearances at hospitals and was snapped by the Courier Mail signing the cast of a twelve-year-old boy at Royal Brisbane Hospital.

Henk Mollee has bittersweet reflections on Best's off-field work for the club. His training clinics were so popular that he feels Brisbane may have left some money on the table.

"[The coaching clinics] were certainly very popular, and other clubs' kids came too, but again it probably wasn't handled well by us because we didn't charge for it. But as I said, it was many years ago and we've learned a lot throughout the years."

It wasn't long before Australian top-flight clubs realised the full marketing potential of guest stars, and they set up exclusive speaking tours and clinics, and only selected them for home games to maximise their gate yield. By the time Kevin Keegan joined Blacktown City in 1985, the promotion of guest stars was completely capitalised.

Five days after his debut, Best faced a rampaging St George side at Perry Park. Reports of Best's performance on debut ranged from okay to world-class, but he was pleased and probably eager to better it after more time on the track with his teammates.

But the new monastic George Best instead faced divine retribution from St George in a 3-0 rout. St George was a top side, and ultimately won the NSL premiership that season. Their younger pros, headed by 19-year-old Robbie Slater who scored the third, descended like a plague of locusts on Brisbane and Best found no space or time on the ball. The first and third goals came directly after Best was dispossessed. David Skeen was first to pinch his pocket and then he beat four Lions tacklers to pound a shot past Nigel Lownds. And Slater's goal, right at the death, was fed by Paul Wilkinson who had just robbed Best of the ball.

Much like the first game, Best was poor in the first half but worked his way into it after the break. Even after the unflattering scoreline, some media outlets found praise for Best's performance, with one description of his second half noting that with his "far more combative attitude, he produced a spray of penetrating passes and many of the sparkling touches expected of him."

But *Soccer Action* had this somewhat circumspect take:

"Guest player George Best was making his second appearance for the home side but failed to produce the match-winning performance for which Lions officials had hoped. In fact, on two occasions that Best was robbed of the ball, St George went on to score."

Although the pundits were hard to please, Best's game did make an impact on his opponents. In an interview in recent years, Slater confessed:

"I was awestruck and you could see how good he'd been."

St George manager Frank Arok, in his last season with the club before taking the Socceroos job, told the media after the game (in an elaborate yet humble brag):

"Best is still a brilliant artist and was at least a class better than the other players on the field. What he proved was that a team motivated as a unit can handle the side that relies on one star player."

Arok's positive description of Best was most likely offered up to the media as a marketing favour to Marconi who were due to face Best in two days' time in the match-up they'd sold the gate for.

"Officially", 3,000 fans attended Marconi's Bossley Park to see Best, but many

A BIT ON THE SIDE (1983)

(McMurdo included) claim a much higher figure. The big crowd pleased everyone, especially Best who reportedly earned $3,000 from his take. But the biggest winner of the day was the marketing manager of Gyprock, the manufacturers of plasterboards. The Lions away kit disappeared on the flight down from Brisbane so they were forced to wear Marconi's away kit for the game. Gyprock, Marconi's shirt sponsor, got a massive freebie on one of Marconi's biggest nights.

The game itself was a fairly dull affair but for one major incident, and it ended 1–1. Vic Bozanic, father of Socceroo Oli, opened the scoring for Marconi before Alan Niven equalised for the Lions in injury time with a penalty.

Alan Niven had also snuck in for the free kick at the edge of the box for Best's opening game against Sydney Olympic. A fullback, Niven only scored 11 times in a stellar 252-game career for the Lions, and he also earned eight Socceroo caps. But two of those 11 goals cost Australian fans the chance to see a George Best goal in the flesh. Perhaps Best didn't want to take penalties or opted not to upset the Lions business-as-usual tactics. But surely a penalty could have been handed to Best to give the fans what they had come to see?

However, no one could really begrudge Niven his chance to score in front of a legend of the game. Tragically, Niven died while playing football (10 years after his retirement from the NSL) at the tender age of 43.

The awarding of that penalty against Marconi required no video assistance. In the dying minutes of the game, Marconi's beloved sweeper and former Socceroo captain, Tony Henderson, decked young Lion Russell Stewart in the box. He was shown a straight red, and Niven converted the spot kick.

Most Marconi fans were bewildered about what had happened. They'd followed the ball and missed Henderson's crime and were looking for answers as he skulked off the field. They'd just sat through 90 dull minutes of football featuring George Best who had put in a poor match.

Alex Vesic in *Soccer Action* was confronting in his assessment of the game:

"Tony Henderson stole the show. It was supposed to be the day of George Best, making his sole Sydney appearance but with Best performing about seven levels below his average, the other [players] took notice and proceeded to dish out just as much rubbish to the disgust of some 3,000 spectators."

Young Marconi midfielder Jovan Djordjevic marked Best and found the going easy—prompting the predictable byline 'Djordevic better than Best'. Best didn't get out of first gear and refused to defend.

He did have a chance to give the Lions the lead before Bozanic's opener. Giant striker Barry Kelso provided Best with a fine lay off at the edge of the box, but he took a few steps, aimed, and fired well past the upright.

David Jack (the third) didn't miss the chance to watch his idol play, even though

Best seemed more like a fallen idol. He recalls that Best had "a quiet match but we didn't care—he was George Best."

He had one game to go on his deal with the Lions the following week against Adelaide City. Before that game, he appeared on the *Parkinson* show on the Thursday night. Best and Parkinson had been friends for decades, starting when Parkinson met a 17-year-old apprentice with United while Parky was doing news on the Manchester-based Granada Television. Parkinson penned an 'intimate biography' of Best in the mid-70s that threatened the friendship, but not irreparably. While in Sydney, Best and McMurdo stayed at Parkinson's place.

Parky was doing his own guest stint in Australia with Channel 10, having stepped away from this eponymous show at the BBC in 1982 and after being let go by ITV's *TV-am* program.

His show was incredibly popular in Australia, and Best was billed alongside Australian TV royalty—Val Lehman who played Queen Bea on *Prisoner*. Parkinson had broken new and weird comedic ground the week before Best's appearance when he had Australian Prime Minister Bob Hawke as a guest alongside impressionist Max Gillies who was a master Hawke impersonator. It was Hawke vs 'Hawke' live on TV, and it was received with mixed reviews. Sydney Morning Herald TV critic Elizabeth Riddell called the Hawke episode "a witless exercise … [and] next week's guests [are] George Best, a soccer has-been and someone from the cast of Prisoner."

Best might have been a "has-been" on the pitch but he wasn't short of material off it. And "someone from Prisoner"? It was Queen Bea! It's probably fair to assume that Ms Riddell was not easily entertained.

After Best walked out to thunderous applause, Parky aired footage of Best scoring six times for United in an FA Cup tie against Northampton in 1970. It's possible that it was the only footage of Best that Channel 10 had, as they had also played it a few weeks earlier in the Tommy Anderson interview. When Best sat down, he remarked with a smirk, "He was a good player that lad, wasn't he?" to the mirth of the audience.

That was the light point of the interview. Parkinson didn't leave anything on the table, probing Best about the mistakes in his career, his drinking, and if he had ever considered suicide. Parkinson was warm, but he didn't go easy on his friend. In fact, it allowed Best to bare all and be brutally honest with the audience who were probably there hoping for some light entertainment. This was a long way from Bob Hawke sending himself up.

PARKINSON: "I never ever thought that you were an alcoholic. I thought of you as a heavy drinker at times, a social drinker, but I never thought of you as an alcoholic but you say you are."

BEST: "You always hide it around friends. I think the longest time I went was 22 days drinking solidly without food. That's when I figured there was a problem."

A BIT ON THE SIDE (1983)

The audience didn't know whether to be shocked, horrified, amused or sympathetic, so they expressed all those responses during the interview.

BEST: "I went through a spell where I couldn't remember anything. There was maybe a week in between where I had a total blackout."

Best talked about rehab and realising with the help of therapists that his drinking sessions were usually sparked by things going well, and not when he was at 'rock bottom'. Indeed, his rock bottoms tended to come with wake-up calls for Best.

Indeed, as Andrew Dettre signposted before his arrival, the Australian trip *was* Best at rock bottom, and so he remained sober to try and let his football speak for him. Because, most importantly, he just wanted to play football.

BEST: "To this day it's still a big love to me. I enjoy it tremendously. I still get a big thrill and, you know, I still feel that buzz when I run onto that field. I know I can do things a little bit special and different to other people, and that excites me. It frightens me that one day it's going to be gone."

So, while Best pondered his football mortality, he had one game left with Brisbane to try and repay their investment and find a bit of the old Best magic.

His final game was against mid-table Adelaide City. But at Richlands in front of 3,600, Adelaide City didn't play like mid-table fodder. They battered the Lions 4–0.

"Brisbane Lions were led to the slaughter," was *Soccer Action's* assessment. "Lions guest star George Best in his farewell appearance for the club was starved of the ball as the visitors controlled midfield play for most of the match."

Ricky Rosso didn't mince words about Best's performance, suggesting that "[Lions manager Simon] Kistemaker… must have had nightmares about Lions bringing George Best back to Australia."

He continued:

"One player Lions can do without on his performance last weekend is 'guest' George Best. After two previous uninspiring performances, Best made promises of turning it on in his final game with Lions. But the former Irish (sic) international succeeded only in turning off the 3,600 who paid to see him and helped to ensure many would not come back.

"Best merely walked around the park, never getting out of [a] trot, never even thinking about a tackle. He didn't get very good service, admittedly, but then he never really worked to get into good positions."

Henk Mollee's review of Best's output for the Lions may have been influenced by his performance against Adelaide City:

"I can only remember him running in the midfield around the circle," he offered as a withering critique of Best.

Goalkeeper Nigel Lownds and teammates believe Best's conditioning played a part too.

"Look, I don't think he was at full fitness. He was [just] in the later stages of his career."

Lownds also played against Bobby Charlton during his brief guest spell at Newcastle in 1978 and compared the two experiences. Two genius players, who had magic in their feet, but who were both limited in what their ageing bodies could achieve on the field.

"George was a 20-minute man," is Lownds' reflective assessment. "But he did what the club wanted and brought the crowds in."

With that match done, Best left Brisbane. He was off to West Adelaide to have another go at the Adelaide City side who had just humiliated him. Best played four games with the Lions, scored no goals and provided no assists. However, he did get the Lions more press coverage than they had received in five years of the NSL and—although the defnitive numbers are debated—crowds swelled while he was in town.

Many people, including Mike Mulvey, remember full houses for the Best matches. Indeed, TV reports included long shots of full and lively grandstands. The fact that the TV news cameras were even present at all was because of Best. To illustrate his allure, in the final match of the 1983 season, the Lions hosted Canberra City at Richlands in front of three *hundred* fans.

Bill McMurdo recalls the Lions being "absolutely thrilled" with Best's commercial return. Henk Mollee, who was on the board, is a little more ambivalent in his assessment:

"For publicity he was good, with the spectators he was good. But we hadn't tied it down well enough. He did other sportsmen's night talks ... for other clubs. That should have come towards (us) and never did. The bad thing was afterward there was a tax issue as well and we ended up having to pay for that. But publicity-wise he did a lot of good, as a lot of people who hadn't been to the football for years came out to see George."

On the field though, it certainly didn't work out. They won once (over Tommy Docherty), pinched a draw against Marconi after a moment of red-time insanity from Tony Henderson, and lost twice, badly.

Keeping their assessment succinct, *Soccer Action* ran a picture of Best in his Lions jersey in their annual 'Boral Bricks Player of the Year' edition. The tagline above the picture read, 'George Best—gained no votes, scored no goals during his guest stint with Brisbane Lions.'

Off the field, Best did leave many cherished memories for teammates, opponents and fans, especially those who attended the Olympic game. Lownds got a photo of his four-year-old son and Best, which still has pride of place in his office today.

To be so close to an icon of the game was also a rare gift that's still cherished by many of Best's teammates.

The Lions ultimately finished bottom of the NSL table in 1983, winning only six times. Simon Kistemaker quit the Lions not long after Best's departure, announcing he had signed on to manage Turnhout in the Belgian Second Division.

"My own standards would suffer if I was involved in Australian soccer too long," Kistemaker was reported as saying when he left Brisbane. "Soccer is my life, but here it is part-time and I doubt soccer will ever be a top sport in Australia."

It wasn't a tearful goodbye for Kistemaker who was almost certainly worn down by the Best experience. And from the bitter tone of the articles about Best's finale with the Lions, so were the football media.

The Belfast Swagman (1983)

After leaving Brisbane, Best headed for Adelaide where he had signed to appear in the 'Plaza Ceramic Challenge Cup' for West Adelaide Hellas. It was an annual friendly with cross-town rivals Adelaide City—the team that had spoiled his Brisbane farewell. He had first played in Adelaide in 1967 but didn't get on the scoresheet in a 5-1 win. He was quoted pre-game in *Soccer Action* as being "happy with his form" and eager to rectify his Adelaide dry spell.

West Adelaide agreed the fee with McMurdo and it covered his and Best's flights and expenses. Hellas won the game 5-3 in front of a packed Hindmarsh grandstand of 5,000 fans.

Like many of his exhibition games without TV cameras, Best's performance in Adelaide has become apocryphal. His efforts for Brisbane against Adelaide City were behind him, and he had the opportunity to extract some revenge playing for West Adelaide. Crucially, he broke his 1983 Australian scoring duck from the penalty spot and is widely discussed as having tormented his opponents all night with his passing range. Today, photos abound of Best with his West Adelaide teammates, and Bill McMurdo still has a keepsake from the game—a West Adelaide Hellas scarf given to him by the club.

In Adelaide he was also photographed with the obligatory Sherrin (an Australian Rules football).

After Adelaide, they jetted west to Perth to play with Osborne Park Galeb. Shortly after they landed in Perth on a dawn flight, McMurdo got a message to call a contact from the Dee Why Football Club in the NSW State Second Division. Waiting for them was an offer and a return trip to Sydney for an exhibition game against the club's local rivals, Manly-Warringah.

"Are you kidding, we've just flown 4,000 miles?" was McMurdo's response.

"Just come, I'll make it worth your while," was the short response from a club representative (whose name McMurdo couldn't recall).

So, Best and McMurdo agreed to give Sydney another go after of course picking up their $8,500 appearance fee with Osborne Park Galeb. Best's deal with Galeb was sometimes reported at the time as two games, but that seems to have been optimistic. He was only ever interested in one, for which Galeb arranged a full package of marketing appearances. The pièce de résistance was 'An Evening with George Best' held at the White Sands Hotel, featuring resident pianist Trevor Pittman and hosted by Gary 'Bongo' Williams.

It was a four-hour marathon broken up by a smorgasbord which included fish, beef stroganoff, or 'seafood' as the hot options. Two thousand fans appeared and McMurdo remembers being "mobbed" at that event. Best had bagged a hat trick on the 1967 tour in front of 20,000 fans in a 7–0 win, so he knew he could draw a crowd in Perth, but neither he nor McMurdo expected that turnout.

However, while the locals adored Best, he was at the end of his tether with the Australian media. At his first press conference in Perth, he was inundated with questions about his off-field exploits. John O'Connell, who was a retired player and the voice of WA football for decades, interrupted the tabloids to say, "George I'm going to ask you a football question," to which Best replied, "Thank Christ for that."

To pay back his kindness, Best offered O'Connell a one-on-one. He lamented to O'Connell that he'd given the last decade of his life to his fans, playing around the world, but had continued to be treated as tabloid fodder. Best was in the country trying to find a path forward out of his addiction. Few journalists stopped to consider that below the headline was a human being.

Best's appearance for Galeb was against Melville Alemania. Galeb had been promoted the season before and were in the bottom half needing a lifeline. Their marketing efforts, including a full- page spread on Best in the Serbo-Croat paper, ensured a sell-out. O'Connell told the ABC that Galeb "had probably 20 or 30 people [normally] watching them on matchday, [and] all of a sudden the ground was packed."

It was a crowd of over 2,000—massive for Galeb. But just like in West Adelaide, his exploits on the pitch have become apocryphal over the years. Galeb won the game 2–1 with Best scoring the opener and setting up the matchwinner. It was the kind of output that the Lions had prayed for, but that Best could only produce on the other side of the country.

Best's goal came very early after going on a run and finding a pocket of space to shoot. There are legends about Best stealing the ball off his teammate (Rodney Marsh-style) before the goal to show everyone who was 'the big dog', but this very likely didn't happen. Bert Kirkpatrick, Best's teammate that day, remembers Best as a man who enjoyed just being part of a team:

"To me, he was very humble, he didn't big-note himself in the dressing room."

This was the same man who probably didn't mind Alan Niven taking the Lions penalty against Marconi—Best probably thought that the stalwart deserved the goal more than he did.

Best's passing range and ball control were lauded at Galeb. O'Connell describes him as "mesmerising the crowd" at times with his ability to control a pass and then play-in a teammate with ease. Best made the second goal possible after he won the ball in a tackle in midfield, then released a teammate out wide with an inch-perfect ball who crossed it in for Johnny Fiamengo to head it home. Suddenly, with a few more games under his belt and more laissez-faire defending than he had received in the NSL, the old Best magic returned.

Perth suited Best. It had been his last stop in Australia in 1967 before jetting home to win the European Cup. He had scored goals in Perth and both the weather and beaches suited him. Best was a mainstay at Scarborough Beach while he was in town and tried to unwind and (unsuccessfully) work on his tan.

According to McMurdo:

"We got to Scarborough and the beach is empty, there is not a fucking soul on the beach. So, we go and put the fucking cream on and are lying there for hours. Pure white the two of us. [But] he could get a tan like that (snaps fingers) and I couldn't understand it."

It was only when a tanned woman from Glasgow pointed out they were using factor 50 sunscreen that the penny dropped.

Best also didn't realise it at the time, but he had just played in his last ever official league match and it was for Osborne Park Galeb. But there was little recognition of this milestone at the time, and there has been very little since. Indeed, a Galeb plaque allegedly given to Best at the time by the club has since been listed and sold on eBay UK with no provenance for the match being Best's last league game.

But he still had one exhibition game left in Australia to show off his newly found form. Best and McMurdo returned to Sydney to stay at the Manly Pacific International and play on the beaches of North Sydney.

Best's fee was reportedly $5,000 to play at Manly-Warringah's Cromer Park, although that figure is disputed, famously by court documents that would surface years later. The game itself was scheduled for the same day that Best was *supposed* to reappear in Bankruptcy Court in London, but McMurdo had that rescheduled so they could earn some extra Australian dollars for the George Best Management Company.

At Dee Why, Best was reunited, again, with the now not-so-young David Jack (the third). Jack had followed Best as a fan, a triallist and now an opponent. Luckily, he had some experience marking Best. In 1970, while Jack was trialling with United, he shared the same training pitch and small-sided training games with Best who was 'carrying' United by then.

Jack's Manchester United experience came, according to him, off the back of his famous grandfather:

"I played for 3 months and they did offer to keep me on for another 12 months but I was homesick. I was only 17, I had a girlfriend back here [in Australia], so I came home. I did play in the B team—they had reserves and first reserves and the A team and the B team—and I played for the B team against Everton and Burnley and Oldham Athletic."

But his admiration for Best never dwindled. While playing for Manly-Warringah, he tried to reenact Best's more famous moments—flicking the ball away from goalkeepers and lobbing them from inside his own half, like Best had done against Spurs in 1970 with a young Jack in the terraces.

"I went through a period of consistently trying the audacious lob that Best pulled off against Spurs at Old Trafford. I gave up shooting with power for a whole season—just lobbed everything. How ridiculous!"

During his trial in Manchester, Jack also tried to reproduce other parts of Best's charm, and he wouldn't be the last victim of celebrity fashion crimes.

"I bought a sleeveless cardigan, which was all the go in 1970, from his boutique—George Best Boutique. I didn't really like the colour and I wore it a few times and I said, 'Can I take it back, George?' and he said, 'OK, but just don't tell them you've worn it.' It was sort of a browny-yellow-mustardy colour. I don't know why I bought it ... I just wanted something from George Best Boutique."

When Best showed up to play with Dee Why, Jack was 30, and he started on the bench for Manly-Warringah. Manly-Warringah players past and present all came out of the woodwork to appear with Best, so Jack magnanimously offered to take a step back. Dee Why is a small club, three beaches up from Manly-Warringah and they are currently plumbing the depths of the National Premier Leagues NSW pyramid. But in 1983, they were in the second tier and their exhibition match with Manly-Warringah was a derby day.

It wasn't an acrimonious rivalry by any means. There had been rumours before 1983 that Manly-Warringah and Dee Why could merge and put together a $150,000 war chest to enter the NSL. That never happened, and the closest thing they got to a permanent bond was their experience hosting George Best.

Up to 5,000 fans packed the hills of Cromer Park to watch Best. This time, Bill McMurdo suited up at fullback for Manly-Warringah. McMurdo often trained with Best, including with the Brisbane Lions, because he never knew when he'd have to (or want to) appear alongside his business partner.

Best came out in an almost fluorescent white Dee Why shirt with the number 11, and he was an apparition against the night sky. And in a way he was, because unlike his performances in Brisbane, he was the ghost of European Cups past on the field that night.

After three minutes, Best, at inside left, intercepted a pass out from the back, flicked the ball up, turned and then lobbed the Manly-Warringah keeper from forty yards. The crowd roared as the Manly-Warringah keeper scrambled back, realising he was about to become a story he could tell his grandchildren before the upright saved him. Best was a millimetre away from scoring one of his greatest ever goals.

The crowd were then offered another cherished memory as a freebie. When Manly-Warringah's Tom Stevens was upended in the box and the referee pointed to the spot, Bill McMurdo stepped up to take the spot kick and slammed it into the crossbar. Today, Jack has no idea how McMurdo was given the responsibility to take the kick—he just picked it up like Paulo Di Canio and marched towards the spot. But unlike with West Ham 15 years later, nobody at Manly-Warringah objected (although they probably wish they had).

Manly-Warringah ultimately did take the lead from a glorious free kick that Best would have been proud of. In the second half, Best *again* found the woodwork. A teammate controlled a hoof forward just inside Dee Why's forward third and prodded it into Best's orbit just outside the box. Best feinted right, then curled a powerful shot with his left that shaved the upright as the Manly-Warringah defence backed off him.

Unlike in his NSL appearances, the crowd and the opponents were hoping he would turn it on and weren't wholeheartedly checking him.

Best opened up his magic bag, dug deep, and tried everything he could find. He dribbled past opponents, sending them one way before doubling back the other. Admittedly, the Manly-Warringah players were doing impressions of witch's hats that would have made Max Gillies proud. But eventually, after so many near misses, Best gave an Australian crowd something they were desperate for—he got on the scoresheet.

His goal made it clear that the linesmen were also invested in him scoring. It was 3-1 to Manly-Warringah approaching the 90-minute mark. With their strong sense of the occasion, Manly-Warringah brought their line up to a laughably high position, nearly into their forward half. Dee Why then pumped a ball over the top for Best to run onto, which he did, taking the ball up to the Manly-Warringah keeper before flicking it over his head and passing it into an open net. 3-2: *despite* Best appearing to be, in David Jack's assessment "miles offside".

He then sent the crowd into delirium. With the 90 minutes almost up, Best collected a short pass from a teammate on the half turn. He went right, slowed, brought the defender to him, feinted a pass, and then poked the ball between his opponent's legs to collect and then take off on a run. The crowd erupted, and his snaking run took him to the edge of the box before he was hacked down.

According to Jack:

"I only came on in the second half. We had about 20 players in the squad and they all wanted to come on. I had a slight hand in one of the goals. I played right midfield or left midfield. I never tackled him—I never tackled anyone actually, which was one of my problems—but I've got some pictures of the game, one where I'm flashing past him."

When the game was up, Best shared a soft drink with his teammates and opponents, declining offers of harder options. He'd had a blinder on the pitch and obliterated all expectations for a midweek friendly. He had also delivered a cherished memory for David Jack. Alas, in a sombre footnote, Jack has lost the picture he took that night with his idol.

The game in Dee Why also brought the club, and Manly-Warringah, a mountain of publicity. The game was telecast (which would never have happened but for Best playing), and reporter Mike Hill spoke with him the following day in the SBS studio. Best looked sleek in a Dee Why-inspired collarless white shirt unbuttoned to his navel—very much a 1970s lothario leaning into the 80s. But the abstinent and battle-worn Best was nervous. He stroked the table between him and Hill nervously like it was Blofeld's cat. He was likely expecting to have his past misdemeanours dredged up again.

Hill stuck to football though, and quickly built a rapport with him. Hill's primary brief was to get Best's feedback on the state of Australian football and footballers. Best's view was in keeping with many guest stars who have been asked the same question:

"I was impressed with quite a few players. A few of the players were disappointing, I think technically more than anything else, which is obviously down to full-time coaching and training."

Best's overall assessment was that the game had a lot of potential but wouldn't reach it until it was fully professionalised. He elaborated:

"The first coaching camp I did with the kids, there were maybe three or four kids who stood out and who really looked good. And out of 80 or 100 kids, that's usually a lot. And I'm talking about comparing myself with kids all over the world, anywhere I've coached."

The challenges arose, he said, when the player reached his teens and could choose to head overseas—as he had from Belfast to Manchester—or stay in Australia.

"Do they stay here and possibly stagnate, or do they go abroad and leave their home country to try and improve?" he posed to Hill. "It's a big decision."

Commendably, Hill ended the interview on a positive note. Rather than point to his past, he asked about Best's future. Best relaxed, smiled, and said he enjoyed coaching kids.

"In the future, that's something I'd like to build up and hopefully at the end of it go into the professional side of it and become a full-time coach possibly … I think a manager and a coach are completely different types of characters. I don't think I'd be equipped to be a manager. I wouldn't have the heart to tell someone I didn't want them anymore. So, I'll stick to coaching."

Best was the eternal child who never lost his appetite to take on players—a skill he decried as being beaten out of prospects in England. He was an evangelist for attacking, exciting football. This spell of sobriety and working with Australian kids had reminded him that he could be the change he wanted to see in the game.

However, Best's match with Dee Why also has a dark stain on it that was not clear to participants at the time. Where Best went, so did money, and where money goes, so do criminals. Best and McMurdo were completely unaware at the time (and since) that part of the money put up for Best's appearance had been embezzled by the two directors of a company called International Commodity Traders Association (ICTA).

Former ICTA President John Maxwell, and vice-presidents Kenneth Smithson and Margaret Goman, were all indicted on fraud charges in 1988 for diverting $1.5 million of investment funds away from the Chicago Mercantile Exchange, and into "private uses". These "private uses" included home renovations and many expensive motor vehicles, but one use cited in court was A$10,000 spent on the organisation of the George Best match (as well as another $50,000 paid as a donation to the Manly-Warringah Soccer Club).

A year after the Best match, ICTA were in deep financial trouble and, according to the *Sydney Morning Herald's* reporting from the District Court, Smithson directed employees to tell investors that their cheques were "in the post", despite the fact a receiver was about to be appointed.

Maxwell and Smithson were ultimately sentenced to six years for fraud and conspiracy after a 15-week trial, and Goman was convicted on a lesser charge of fraud.

It is a grave footnote to Best's 1983 tour, and one largely forgotten. However, it serves as a poignant reminder that the money swirling around football, and some that found its way into Best's pocket, is not always clean.

At his peak – George Best in a promotional shot for Manchester United, Christmas 1969. His former girlfriend Eva Haraldsted (centre) is standing behind him.

Best sipping tea before a press conference on arrival at Sydney Airport in 1983

Best with the Cup to commemorate his stint with West Adelaide, 1983

Best with talk show host (Sir) Michael Parkinson, 1983

Best with the inevitable photo with a 'Sherrin' – the brand of spherical 'ball' used in Australian Rules Football, 1983

Best with the Osborne Park (Perth) team, 1983

Best in a promotional shoot for the popular soccer newspaper of the time, 'Soccer Action', 1983 (Photo: Laurie Schwab Collection)

Best heading to Her Majesty's prison after an appeal against a drink driving charge failed, 1984.

The full photograph from the cover shot shows Best with three Marconi Under-8 players (L-R): Denis Rapiti and brothers Nahuel and Ismael Arrarte, 1989

Denis Law and Best in a promotional shot for the charity match to aid Lidcombe Hospital in Sydney, 1990

Best with Rodney Marsh with their video Drugs, Mugs & Thugs about the 1994-95 Premier League season.

Authors Jason Goldsmith (L) and Lucas Gillard outside Crazy Pedro's Pizza - formerly Best's fashion boutique known as George Best Edwardia - on a visit in 2022

The Inter Years (1984-1988)

Best was barely on the plane before the media completely turned against him. There were dissenting voices from the start—namely from Dettre—over his fee, but other than unfriendly match reports, journalists tended to either write about the playboy or the former star who was on a football goodwill tour.

Rale Rasic was an early dissenter:

"Was George Best the right type of 'super star' to bring over for a guest stint? Let's face it, his football days were over, and with the Lions he turned out to be nothing more than 'Mr Ordinary'."

Johnny Warren also partially blamed Best for the Lions terrible overall season.

Best had obviously had enough. Bill McMurdo had arranged a three-match deal with Christchurch Mogal United in New Zealand after the Australian tour, but then sought to introduce a "no media contact" clause into the deal or else threatened not to honour it. The Christchurch board weren't impressed. Without media work and the associated attention, what was the point? Best never joined Christchurch, and instead returned home to London to visit an old acquaintance—Bankruptcy Court.

The 1983 tour could hardly be considered a 'success' for Best. Financially there had been wins, but this tour was about more than money. He wanted his football to talk for him to remind the world who he was on the pitch and to forget everything off it. Alas, his performances couldn't silence the media scrutiny about George Best the drunk, George Best the womaniser and George Best the man who had pissed his talent away. He chose to walk into the colosseum, sober, to face his lions and serve his penance to football. But those lions couldn't be charmed.

In the months after his Australian sojourn, Best was at a career intersection. He conceived a series of fitness records with Mary Stavin called *Shape Up and Dance* which involved him—allegedly—doing a nude photo shoot.

As far as concept albums go, *Shape Up and Dance* is an interesting one. Designed as an aerobics aid, Best fans are encouraged to pop on a leotard, spin the record and follow an eight-page exercise guide.

Best and Stavin's effort was part of the Shape Up and Dance franchise which also released albums hosted by stars like Lulu and Felicity Kendall. It's a mixture of songs like the Marvin Gaye song 'It Takes Two', later immortalised by Tina Turner and Rod Stewart, where one presumes Best is singing the male part with the obvious support of auto-tune. In between, upbeat tracks are fitness routines between Best and Stavin where they commentate on their moves for the listener. "Put your legs together and stretch toward my chest," he directs Stavin, presumably lunging towards him while a session musician sings 'Just the Two of Us'.

As far as musical careers go, Best wasn't in a position to give up his day job. His apprehension years before about a concept album with Rodney Marsh seemed correct, but the Best of 1983 ignored (or wasn't in a position to ignore) the inner voice reminding him he couldn't sing.

To get back to football, Best assembled the 'George Best XI' who picked up exhibition games around the world, and the team included legendary names like his former Fulham teammates Bobby Moore and Rodney Marsh, as well as Gordon Banks and Alan Ball, and as the 1980s went on, Kevin Keegan. And of course, Bill McMurdo at fullback. They would visit places like Hong Kong or Dubai and pick up three or four matches in a month.

Best's former teammates and opponents loved being selected to play in exhibition games with him. Many approached him for autographs for themselves but were too shy to admit it and claimed they were asking on behalf of their wives.

According to manager Bill McMurdo:

"I suppose that is the best praise you can get if your fellow footballers or fellow professionals held you up there. He got that everywhere he went, he was treated with absolute respect."

McMurdo believes Best made more money picking up exhibition games around the world than he, or anyone, could have made starring in the English First Division at that time.

And during periods of sobriety, Best kept himself fit and ready for action by running miles and genuinely enjoying training.

"The reason he survived for so long I believe is because he was a great trainer," recounted McMurdo. "If you got him on the pitch, he was always the first one on the pitch and the last to leave. He was a bit of a fitness freak in some ways. Not many people saw that side of him. You couldn't play that type of game and not be fit. His fitness got him through a lot. He was always fit."

While he didn't appear in New Zealand in 1983, he did appear against the New Zealand national side a year later in an exhibition game playing for Reading alongside Martin Peters in front of nearly 4,000 fans in a 2–1 loss.

THE INTER YEARS (1984-1988)

It was one of Best's first games of football after being released from Pentonville Prison. He served 56 days for drunk-driving offences and assaulting a policeman who had been sent to ensure he appeared in court. These crimes from November 1983 are proof that his Australian sobriety didn't hold. In true Australian tabloid style, in their report of Best's arrest the *Canberra Times* article ran the line, 'What would his old teammate Bobby Charlton say?'

When he was sentenced, Best famously remarked, "Well, I suppose the knighthood's fucked." On his charge sheet, he listed his profession as 'unemployed'. He was sentenced to 90 days in Pentonville but was released after just over half that time.

But it shouldn't have come to that. Best was told to plead guilty in exchange for the judge offering a fine. But Best had other ideas and, like he had on the pitch, he tried to improvise. McMurdo explains:

"George said, 'What happens if I go to jail?' I said, 'You're not going to get jail, the judge has agreed. If you plead guilty ... you will get a heavy fine.' He says, 'Fuck it, Bill, I'm going to plead not guilty and then my case won't be heard until next year, so I'll be out for Christmas.' He didn't want to be in jail for Christmas. So, I said, 'George, do me a favour, don't be so fucking daft.' He said, 'No, Bill, I'm pleading not guilty.' He gets up there and pleads not guilty and the normal procedure would have been to call the case two or three months down the road, but [the judge] went and fucking called the case for the following Monday, didn't he. So, he ended up getting three months. I said, 'You should have listened, the deal was done. You're fucking going to be in prison now for Christmas.'"

At the time, McMurdo told the press, "If it had been you or me, he would probably have got off with a fine. I believe he suffered because of who he is, because he is a public figure."

But privately, McMurdo knew the grave mistake his friend had made.

His wife, Angie Best, who frequently appeared in the media defending George despite them having been separated for a long time, likened his imprisonment to "caging a lion—he's such a free spirit. But it will give him time to reflect, to look at his life. It may sound a wicked and hard thing to say, but maybe he needs his freedom taken away from him to give him that chance. I'm not worried about him in jail. It will do him more good than harm."

However, Best perceived threats around every corner. He was nervous about prison life (based on its reputation) but found himself instantly on his feet. McMurdo visited him after his first night to find Best in better spirits than he anticipated.

"'I was fucking petrified, Bill,' he said. 'I was lying in the cell last night and there's a knock on the cell door ... Next thing the fucking door opens. I go to the door and there's a cup of cocoa and a fucking Mars bar left from supper. I don't know who it was from or whatever, but I enjoyed it and was feeling a bit better.'"

The next morning while he showered, Best was approached by another inmate. "He was having a shower and this guy comes up to him and says, 'George I want you to meet so-and-so and he says he wants to meet you now,'" McMurdo recalls.

McMurdo either withheld the identity of the prison kingpin, or it wasn't shared with him: but safe to say, he would have been the kind of character who demanded instant attention. McMurdo continues:

"He gets taken to this guy and this guy is in charge of the prison. He says, 'George, I don't know you. I don't know anything about football, I've never seen football in my life, I don't know who you are or whoever but they tell me that you're a genuine guy,' he says. 'I'm prepared to back you on that,' and he says, 'All the time that you are here, you won't have any problem at all, whether that be wardens or prisoners. Any problems, you come and see me.' He was looked after. That put his mind at rest, as you can imagine."

Prison also turned out to have a silver lining. During the time he was there, Best was supposed to be in India playing a series of charity matches. Instead, when he was released, The George Best XI picked up a game against Best's old inmate team at Pentonville. They drew a crowd of over 2,000 people.

Rats in the Ceiling (1989)

When George Best returned to Australia at the end of the decade, he wasn't the same man that departed in 1983. He was drinking again but had made peace with the fact that his football skills now belonged in exhibition matches, not league matches for premiership points. And he was enjoying football again.

He knew his time at the top was up. And his time at the bottom was proving even more lucrative. Jet-setting around the world to pick up matches was proving to be both fun and a real money spinner.

Indeed, between 1983 and 1989, his cycle of heavy drinking followed by sobriety spiralled. McMurdo's role during this time was part manager, friend, housemate and, sometimes, bodyguard.

"When he was stone-cold sober, we would have guys coming up sending over bottles of champagne and he would send them back and say, 'Look, thanks, but I'm not drinking.' 'Is my fucking money not good enough for you?' they'd say and want to fight him. I would tell them, 'Look, don't take it personally, he's not drinking.' They thought that they had been slighted and wanted to fight him."

Long periods of sobriety like that in 1983 were not uncommon for Best, according to McMurdo:

"He could go for 6 months at a time and not touch a drink, not even feel like it from what he told me. Different times, he would have a run and have no drink and he would be enjoying life. In '87 in particular, he spent a lot of time [not] really drinking at all. We had a flat together … and there were times when he could handle it quite well and there were other times where he couldn't handle it."

McMurdo says Christmas was a difficult time for Best, and often a trigger. But there were others too. Reflecting on his past success was another.

"His wife, Angela, told me … when he was in San Jose, he had been sober for about a year and he went to this football thing, this football dinner and he was presented with an award with 1,000 people there. Presented with an award for his contribution to football and he went fucking missing after it, missing for a week, drinking."

Best often spiralled into drink when things were going well in his life. But when he was at his lowest, he would turn to sobriety.

McMurdo reflects:

"I saw the signs most of the time. He would get grumpy about different things and I would think, '*He wants a fucking drink.*' He would say to me, 'Let's run through the itinerary, let's run through my diary.' You could see his mind going.

"I remember one time ... We lived in the Barbican in London at the time and I just came up the road and I got a phone call on a Saturday morning and Angie says to me, 'You need to come down.' So, we got down, I'll never forget, there's fucking thousands of wee flats. Anyway, I get down there and I can't get in and there's a wee windowpane next to the door and I can see him lying there. I thought he was fucking dead. I'm banging the door and nothing."

Eventually McMurdo got the door open and woke Best up. He was alive, but very drunk.

"So, I woke him up eventually. I gave him a couple of sleeping tablets and put him back to sleep and stayed there for a couple or three days and every time he woke up, I gave him a couple of sleeping tablets until we got out whatever was in his system."

McMurdo then suggested to Best that he get out of London for a while and stay in McMurdo's house in Glasgow. Before heading to Heathrow for the flight, they stopped in a restaurant in Piccadilly for hamburgers and tea. McMurdo knew something was off.

"So, George is sitting there, and he's got this look about him. I knew he is not fucking right. All of a sudden, the guy brings two hamburgers and puts them down and George says to me, 'Back in a minute, I'm going to the toilet.' He fucking bolted, didn't he. Straight through the door. I couldn't do anything, could I. Sat there, two meals. He wasn't even coming to Scotland, he just fucked off."

When McMurdo got through as much of his two hamburgers as he could manage, he left the restaurant and paused momentarily to notice a familiar face in the window of the pub across the road.

"I say, 'What the fuck are you playing at?' He says, 'I'm sorry, Bill, I just needed a drink, I can't order a drink in front of you. It upsets me.' I said, 'George, all you had to do was tell me that you're needing a drink, if you're needing a drink then fucking take a drink rather than fucking leaving me.'"

Best and McMurdo did make their way to Glasgow soon afterwards for a couple of pleasant, sober months.

While drinking often interfered with their lives, McMurdo's fraternal bond with Best saw them through.

"All said though, [for] every bad time I had with him, there was 1,000 good times."

Around this time, Best visited Dubai for an exhibition game that didn't exactly go to plan. That wasn't uncommon for Best, but this time it was McMurdo's fault, when

RATS IN THE CEILING (1989)

he *accidentally* two-footed a Prince.

According to McMurdo:

"So, the game has two minutes to go and it was an AstroTurf. I see this guy fucking running through right and they're all fucking laying off him, he's fucking running through. I thought '*Fuck this*,' and I went after him, and bang! I took him down just outside the box. Next thing all these fucking soldiers are running on the pitch with all these fucking guns at me—'Fucking don't move!' I didn't know the guy I brought down was a fucking Prince. All of the guys had been told to lay off him because of his position but no one had told me, so I fucking put him up in the air."

McMurdo and Best smoothed things over later that night at a banquet at the palace … Or so it seemed.

"[Later] we were to go to Dubai to speak at a dinner like two years after it. We had to apply for visas and my visa got knocked back. They wouldn't give me a visa. I said, 'Fuck it, George, let's go anyway and we'll take a chance. What's the worst, they send me back to London?' Eventually they agreed to let me in for the dinner—this big prestigious dinner him and I were speaking at. I had to leave at five o'clock in the morning. I had this visa until five o'clock in the morning … because of that guy that I didn't know who he was. I just threw him up in the air which was normal."

Trouble had a way of finding Best, even when he didn't court it. Even in the most remote places on the football map.

Best also, too often, found trouble in very public places—like the BBC. He signed on to be a key player in the BBC's coverage of the Mexico 1986 World Cup, a tournament featuring his home nation of Northern Ireland. But he failed to appear at the studio for Northern Ireland's first game against Algeria, forfeiting his $10,000 payment for the four weeks of the tournament.

"My decision is my decision and mine alone," Best said at the time. His role was given to his countryman Martin O'Neill.

"I saw George about a week ago and all I can say is he's up to his old tricks again," was the only light his estranged wife, Angie, could cast on the situation when contacted by the media.

By 1988, Best and McMurdo's working relationship had come to an end. McMurdo told *The Sun* at the end of '88 that Best was "drinking himself to death" by "sinking 24 glasses of champagne a day plus vodka and Bacardi cocktails."

Best reportedly denied his former partner's claims by saying, "OK, so I go out and have a drink … [but] my liver is not shot to pieces. I'm in good shape."

It was a public fallout, but one that McMurdo doesn't carry any scars over today. Best was a dear friend, and while they no longer held a professional relationship, he would always be a brother to him.

In 1989, at the venerable age of 43, Best returned to Australia for 'The Best Australian

Tour'. He had been able to put a lot of his financial troubles behind him after playing in his own testimonial match at Windsor Park in Belfast. And now with McMurdo no longer by his side, his life partner Mary Shatila was also acting as his business partner.

They were approached by a fellow Belfast boy, Billy Millen, to tour Australia once more.

Millen had grown up with Best in Belfast—Best once scored seven goals in a youth game against Millen, and their careers deviated early on once the relative skill of the two young men became apparent. Millen went onto Linfield, where according to the *Belfast Telegraph*, he "terrorised defences and scored goals for fun".

Millen was the architect of one of Northern Ireland's greatest football nights when he scored both goals in a 2-1 home win against Manchester City in the 1970 Cup Winners' Cup.

However, to leave the troubles in Belfast behind, Millen explored new opportunities, first in South Africa and then Australia. His landing point was Marconi where his football pay was supplemented with a job in the club rooms.

"Yeah, they gave me a job at the Marconi club," says Millen, "and everything was written in Italian. I said, 'Oh what have I come to?'"

Millen also quickly wondered what he had walked into off the pitch, and what terrors might be lurking in the clubrooms.

"I said, 'Lads, there's an awful sound in the ceiling.' So, I popped the ceiling. I thought it was possums. It was not, it was rats. You should have seen the size of them. Oh, my goodness, they were like cats."

Millen's career at Marconi hit a crossroads when Rale Rasic stepped in as manager. He wasn't getting a look-in, and the money he had been offered wasn't always provided as promised. So, he left for Sydney Croatia where, after two games, he broke his ankle at a wedding.

"I said, 'I can't get to training. What about my money?' They said, 'That's your problem. You get here.' I said, 'It's rather hard to get to training with a broken ankle.' So, that never lasted all that long," reflected Millen.

Difficulty getting paid was a recurring theme in Millen's Australian career. It was a lesson he never forgot when negotiating deals for Best. He expected to bump into Australian football rats in management as well as in ceilings.

Millen ensured he was paid upfront for Best's appearance fees in 1989.

"It was $3,000 a night [for clubs to book Best], so once it got to 10, I was like, 'George, here's $30,000.'"

Best had 18 appearances in total, and Millen earned his money from the other eight.

The tour was sponsored by Nordmende TV because Millen worked there and he talked his bosses into the deal.

"I said to the boss, 'Maybe bring Bestie out, and we'll do brochures with photographs and all.' So, it was good that way."

Also sponsoring the tour were Australian Airlines, Philomena Travel Service, Ray Richards 4R's Sports Factory and the Southern Pacific Hotel Corporation.

Best's first stop on his 1989 tour wasn't quite a 'theatre of dreams'. It was King Village, a hotel and spa in Wantirna, east of Melbourne. An ad for King Village adorns the inside cover of the official tour program, featuring a blonde model right out of the Best playbook, along with the tagline: 'King Village, the Best way to mix business and pleasure ... At the end of the day, George needs to relax and that is why he chose to stay at King Village.'

The King Village Club was also the site of Best's first speaking gig. The next day he crossed the bay to the Geelong Soccer club, where a football writer named Michael Lynch was among the crowd. In an article in *The Age* years later, Lynch claimed Best was half an hour late after requiring a detour via a local pub. But when Best showed up, he was great value.

According to Lynch, "He made plenty of soccer training videos and was asked why he did not make one about his love life. 'They only last an hour and a half,' he quipped."

The next day, Best was booked to play in a charity match at the home of the Doncaster Rovers Soccer Club, based in the north-eastern suburbs of Melbourne. The match was organised by the Melbourne chapter of the Celtic Supporters Club to raise money for the Biala School for Disabled Children.

It was a 'Celebrity XI' vs 'Australian XI' match with an international cast. Willie Wallace and Terry Hennessey played (both were in the country coaching), and several other former Australian internationals and NSL legends took part.

The match also featured another 'big' Australian football name. A handy amateur player named David Hill, then chairman of the ABC (and soon to become chairman of the Australia Soccer Federation).

As ASF chairman, David Hill oversaw the creation and expulsion of five NSL franchises. But in 1989, he was a little more circumspect, telling ABC TV:

"George Best, for about a decade, produced things in soccer we'll never ever see again. I'm out of my depth here."

Crowd reports varied from the hundreds to over a thousand. But they were all treated to a thrilling match, especially in the second half. Best scored after a driving run and then got another from the penalty spot in the final moments in a seven-goal thriller. The match raised $10,000 for the Biala School.

Victorian Soccer Federation chairman Joe Docherty gave a rousing team talk to the 22 players, telling then ABC chairman David Hill, "We've received a transfer request, you start at Channel 7 on Monday," to raucous applause.

After the game, Best was asked by ABC TV if he had any difficulties getting himself ready to play. He replied, "I've never had any problem with that. Whether it's a kick around with kids, or a game like this, or a proper First Division, they're all the same. I enjoy them all."

It was a line that spoke so much of his lifestyle and involvement in the game after leaving Manchester United.

Best claimed it was his 600th exhibition game, which underlined just how many miles were in his legs by this stage. But it also demonstrated how Best's story was interwoven with Australian football. He knew many of his teammates and saw the match as a chance to catch up with old friends and generate some funds for a great cause.

Best was also asked if the people of Melbourne would see him again.

"I hope so," Best replied. "I love it here and we've received a few offers. There's a lot of expats here ... it's like coming home really ... It's almost certain I'll be back at some stage."

Alas, there was so nearly another living legend on the pitch that night. Ferenc Puskás, who was coaching South Melbourne in the NSL, was booked to play, but according to Millen (in a somewhat apocryphal version of events), Puskás was turned away by an overly officious Doncaster official.

"The guy asked him, 'What's your name?' He said, 'Puskás,' and the guy said, 'Aye, and I'm John Wayne, fuck off.' But he was the real Puskás!"

Video footage of Puskás in the rooms after the game shows he was there, albeit not in a playing strip.

It was the experience of a lifetime for Best, who idolised Puskás. He considered the Real Madrid duo of Di Stefano and Puskás to be his all-time favourites. Later, Best jumped at the opportunity to lunch with Puskás, and the meal proved memorable to Millen for other reasons.

"I've never seen anybody eat as many meatballs in all my life," remembers Millen of Puskás. "I would have done that for about two weeks. He had forty meatballs."

After the match, Best headed to the small city of Traralgon on the way to Gippsland in Victoria. A throng of kids awaited him after a clinic at Traralgon City's club rooms. Best greeted them all with autographs, personalised notes and photos. That night, he spoke before 200 of their parents about "his career, his opponents, his sexual conquests, his alcoholism [and] his prison term for drink-driving and assaulting the police".

Martin Flanagan of *The Age* described his openness as "gentle ... subtly Irish, often leaving questions as artfully as he once left defenders."

Best was so practised in the after-dinner circuit that he could effortlessly slip into character, and he tended to not rule topics out of bounds because, sadly, there wasn't a corner of his life that hadn't already been illuminated by the media. All Best could do was to smile and embrace the character the audience wanted him to be while they finished their dessert.

"Only when he sat down did one sense the price he paid for being George Best, the tension of the performer whose fame is such that he is never allowed to leave the stage," is how Flanagan put it.

When asked, Best provided glimpses into the importance of tours like this Australian one. He had achieved the heights of his sport in 1968 and would never reach them again. However, staying in football was the microdose he needed to stay connected to the Best at the top of his game, and what he once was.

"I tried to find it in drink and that didn't work. You think it does for a while but then you have to face it the next day and it's worse. I try to do it now through things like this [Traralgon]—coaching kids, playing in exhibition games. The buzz is not the same, but perhaps that is age, learning to be satisfied with less potent experiences."

Although Best was drinking while on the tour, he was also delivering to crowds. This was very much Best the functioning alcoholic, who was drinking but meeting his obligations. But away from audiences, Best was struggling. Millen, Best and Mary Shatila crossed the border from Victoria to New South Wales a couple of times on this tour, and into the ACT. On one drive from Melbourne, Best begged Millen to stop at a pub near the Murray River so he could get a drink.

Later on the tour at Marconi, Best was interviewed by football journalist Mike Cockerill of the Sydney Morning Herald:

"I spend more time these days in the air than on the ground." Best charmed Cockerill in a similar way to Flanagan.

"Certainly, few who have met Best have come away disappointed," Cockerill noted.

Both journalists walked away from their engagements having observed a humble and generous man who was happy to spend hours after training clinics signing autographs and having pictures taken.

Best, the entertainer, had wowed hungry audiences at Marconi, and the Randwick-Coogee RSL Club.

Best, the boy from Cregagh, also found joy through being on training pitches coaching Marconi's under 8s.

The tour was proving to be a success for all parties before the crew headed for South Australia and stops at the Whyalla and Adelaide Soccer Clubs.

When he arrived at Adelaide Airport, Best signed Manchester United jerseys and shared stories with "dozens" of press (including the *Adelaide Advertiser*) and TV media who awaited him. He told them, perhaps foolhardily, that he'd caught wind of Fleet Street offering Australian paparazzi money for lurid photos of him.

"It's unbelievable, isn't it, but it's true" he told reporters, who must have contemplated their own possible pay days. When one of throng asked him if he was still a drinker, he replied "These days I drink for pleasure, not to get drunk."

It was a derivation of a line Best had used before, and one that was likely code for "not in the midst of a multi-day bender." Indeed he drank during the 1989 tour, but never to the point of missing engagements; which was also a common trend in Best's life.

His Adelaide trip included a luncheon at the Travelodge, which for a while, threatened to turn into an international incident when "a handful of Pommy yobos" (as they were oddly described by the media) cheered and jeered and made "inane comments" throughout the sold-out event. But handling "Pommy yobos" was all in a day's work for George Best. He pacified the crowd delivered another memorable evening.

However, as was common in Best's life, the relative normalcy of his tour to that point would prove to be too good to be true.

After his midweek appearances, Best ventured to the Adelaide Casino on a Friday night. According to reports at the time, he lost "thousands" of dollars at the roulette table. Other sources alleged Best "won $10,000 one night, then lost $18,000 the next night".

But as alleged by *Adelaide Advertiser* journalist Peter Hackett, Best did not take his losses well. The following week, newspapers reported that Hackett was suing Best for $100,000 in damages for a savage assault that occurred in the toilets of the Casino. Allegedly, Best had caused "severe bruising to the head and lower left leg and concussion" to the journalist, all—as claimed by Hackett in his court writ—because the journalist recognised the former player and said, "G'day George."

Hackett claimed in court that he had been "repeatedly kicked, dragged into a cubicle and then punched".

Crucially, Hackett took the step to pursue a civil suit after police did not press charges. "Soccer sources" (whomever they might be) told the Sydney Morning Herald that no one could corroborate Hackett's account, and that two witnesses told police, "Nothing had happened."

Best was interviewed twice by police and then allowed to leave Adelaide. Criminal charges were never made against him despite a month-long investigation, and the civil suit also ultimately disappeared into the ether.

When the media caught the story, Millen went into damage control.

"I had to hide him for three days," Millen recalls, also confirming that Best had lost a sizeable amount of money at the Casino.

After this short hiatus, Best next headed to Sydney, where Millen sought new events to add to the itinerary. Time was money, and Best by all accounts needed it.

"George Best for Lunch" was hastily organised for the Camperdown Travelodge. Twenty-three dollars included wine, a three-course meal, and a chance to ask Best "anything you want, and a chance to get him to autograph almost anything."

The plug for the event was in the 'Our Town' section of the Sydney Morning Herald, listed beneath a 'Martini Mixing Competition'. While Best was front page news in most parts of the world, alas for Sydney socialites, his dry wit could not compete with a dry martini. Or perhaps, this 'slow news' story was Millen trying to continue Best's low profile in the wake of the Adelaide Casino story.

After Sydney, Best went south for a final match in Tasmania. Here, Best reunited with another former Manchester United graduate who had made Tasmania his home. Ken Morton is considered a coaching legend in Australian football, having coached Newcastle and Wollongong in the top-flight before establishing himself in Tasmania. He also worked in Malaysia, Vietnam and Ethiopia before settling permanently in Tasmania.

As a 1960s kid, he followed Best's footsteps in the United Academy, but had to look elsewhere for playing time and joined York City.

But he will never forget playing beside Best and his other heroes at United training.

"I played with him in the A team, the B team and the youth team. We scored bags of goals together. When we played together, we were a good partnership, we complemented each other."

In 1989, Morton was in charge of Devonport City where Best would play and face a Tasmanian State rep side. In front of 1,800 supporters, Best's smallest yet in Australia, Best put on one of his finest shows.

Before the game, he put on a literal clinic for local elite teens, before turning his attention to the game. Local football journalist Walter Pless followed Best's movements in Tasmania as a Matthew or Mark would have followed Christ:

"Best, who had lingered in the bar of the club's lavish new facilities at Valley Road, seemed unhurried as he made his way to an empty corner [of the dressing room]. He winked at a photographer, then sat down to begin his match preparations which appeared to lack any kind of superstitions. He casually posed for photographs, signed books, posters, soccer balls and scraps of paper."

There was palpable excitement in the air for kick-off, but it almost ended in disaster inside the first few minutes. The local hard man, a Geordie named David Crosson, slid into Best and sent him flying.

As Best writhed in the dirt, Morton screamed at Crosson, "If he goes, there's no game!"

But Best got up and played on, with a chastened Crosson content with his one shot at glory.

Despite his swollen knees and conspicuous paunch, Best hadn't lost any of his touch. He created the first goal after his thunderous shot was parried out into the path of Devonport striker Androny Rimmer. Then Best set up the second goal with a textbook through-ball for Rimmer to score.

Best was dropping 30-yard passes on a penny, and got out all his old tricks, like playing the ball off his opponent's shins as he once had for United.

The game ended 2-2 and he had delighted fans. Afterwards, hidden away from any paparazzi or Fleet Street goons, Best cleaned the mud off his own boots and then downed a can of beer before hitting the showers.

After the game, football journalist Walter Pless asked Best who was the greatest player of all time.

"I was," Best answered. "Pelé said so, and he should know."

Then Best did something he couldn't bring himself to do in 1983. He drank with his teammates.

Morton helped cater for the afterparty by asking Mary Shatila about Best's favourite drink. Her answer was Moet-Chandon, so Morton put the order in at the local pub for two dozen bottles, and they dutifully arranged them.

After a few celebratory cans, the team headed to the pub to keep the night going. Around midnight, some locals (including the publican) sought a game of snooker with Best in another room. That was the last time Morton saw Best that night.

The next day, Morton learned that the snooker game had turned into an all-nighter, and that only one Moet-Chandon bottle remained. To his credit, the publican (who played snooker all night with a living legend), never charged Morton for the Moet.

Best loved Tasmania. It reminded both him and Millen of Belfast in its own way. But even thousands of miles from home, Best was always recognised.

"I remember one day going to a remote island off Tasmania and betting George $20 no-one would know him there. We got off at Green Island and walked up like 100 yards, and there was the president of the Rangers supporters club in Melbourne. He said, 'Hello, George, how are you?' George said, 'Where's my 20 bucks?' He couldn't go anywhere."

Millen didn't have many problems with Best in 1989. Indeed, he would not give air to the alleged incident at the Casino. However, there was one incident on a plane:

"First time, I tell you, he was well-behaved. The only thing was one time we had a few jars at the airport. It was funny. He went to jump over me to get to the toilet and there he is flying in first class. He was like a dead spider and we were killing ourselves laughing. If you had mobile phones in those days, I'm sure somebody would have sold it."

The Best Australian Tour officially ended in Devonport, but he and Millen extended the tour to return to South Australia, according to the press, "by popular demand". The heat from the Casino incident had dissipated, and Best was drawn back to Adelaide on the offer of another exhibition game.

At Ramsay Park in Elizabeth, Best would line up for the George Best XI vs the Sam Service (the Northern Irish former South Melbourne and West Adelaide goalkeeper) XI to raise money for a young Para Hills footballer who had suffered a serious leg injury two years earlier and had to have part of his leg amputated. An opposition tackle to the shin had caused both bones and the main artery to be severed, and the player in question had to be hospitalised for 22 days.

That player was Neil Fuller, who would go on to have an illustrious paralympic career. He won six Paralympic Golds throughout his athletic career, including four in Sydney in 2000, and has also been awarded the Order of Australia.

The money raised by the Best charity game was used to help fund Fuller to compete for Australia in the 1989 FESPIC games in Japan, which was a key step in Fuller's athletic career, which then took him to a Long Jump Bronze in the 1990 World Championships, and then a relay Gold and then Two individual Silvers and a Bronze at the Barcelona Paralympics.

Best could not have foreseen any of Fuller's future success, but did see an opportunity to help and do what he loved: play football.

Celtic legend and Lisbon Lion Willie Wallace, who was living and coaching in Sydney flew to Adelaide to play, and joined a mix of British and Irish stars including Dundee's and West Adelaide's Alby Kidd, former Socceroo Jim Muir, and Morton's Martin Doak who is the grandfather of current Liverpool teenager (and Celtic academy graduate) Ben Doak. Tim White, the then Victorian Director of Coaching, also flew over for the opportunity. Billy Millen followed in Bill McMurdo's footsteps and arranged a cap for himself.

Before gameday Best was invited back to the Travelodge to entertain another luncheon crowd. The $30 three-course meal tickets were sold out immediately, and attendees were treated to more of Best's exploits on and off the pitch. But there was another good reason to attend: one lucky guest - allegedly - won the chance to play in the charity match Best was about to suit up in.

He was so popular with Travelodge staff at this point, that he was to wear a custom-made Travelodge jersey for the event.

A couple of days later at Ramsay Park in Elizabeth, Best and friends put on a show. Accompanied in the warm up by "Jimmy Queentin's Irish dancers" and the "Ballantines Scotch Pipe band". The reported 3000 attendees caught a thoroughly memorable 6-6, in which Best scored from the penalty spot. Crowds roared as Best touched the ball, and kids spilled out to sit by the pitchside to watch the legend in the flesh. The game was so big that the SA Amateur League agreed to postpone games around it.

The game is perhaps best known today for the appearance of Best in the hoops of Celtic FC. Something must have gone wrong with the promised Travelodge jerseys, as by kick-off Best and his team, which included Celtic legend Willie Wallace, were in the famous white and green.

And while it was played at a pace befitting the age of the players, it was a fitting way for Best to end his 1989 tour. A leisurely game of football, in front of thousands who cheered and sang him on throughout, with thousands more Australians on the tour entertained by him both on and off the pitch.

Indeed the end of 1989, there was plenty of affection for Best in Australia. A public poll was run to name outgoing Socceroo coach Frank Arok's replacement. While Arok himself won the poll (which was odd, as Arok had left the post), Best finished alongside Brian Clough as the preferred "international" options.

In dollar terms, it seems a little easier to measure his impact. SBS approached Best to be a special pundit for their coverage of the 1990 World Cup. Johnny Warren, with a hint of sour grapes, used his regular article 'Warren on Soccer' in the Sydney Morning Herald to tell his readers that Best asked for $120,000 plus expenses for the month-long gig.

Clearly the SBS hadn't checked the 'news' of what Best was up to during the 1986 tournament, nor the much more amenable $10,000 he was willing to be paid by the BBC. Inflation can be serious but, if Warren's article is accurate, one can only assume that Best wasn't very keen on the job and picked a figure he'd be willing to get serious for.

Law and Disorder (1990)

The 1989 tour had gone well enough for Best. There was the unpleasantness at the Adelaide Casino, including some lost funds, but generally he had given himself to his fans and taken out some joy as well (as well as a good amount of cash).

1989 had been such a hit that Best was, reportedly, contemplating settling in Australia permanently. *The Mail* reported in January of 1990 that Best had "left Britain for good" and was seriously contemplating relocation.

"I've got stacks of work offers," Best told People. "Down under, I've been approached to do sports catalogue modelling."

It was also fortuitous that this 1990 urge to leave Britain also coincided with the release of his autobiography, (which was ultimately called) *The Good, The Bad and the Bubbly*, which threatened to burn some bridges or two.

"There could be a few folk after me," Best told the media in the lead-up to the book's release.

Best had a lot riding on his book, and there were rumours circulating at the time that he had arranged for the movie rights to be sold, and that Mel Gibson was being lined up to play him. Sadly, the Mel Gibson-Best biopic has not been forthcoming and seems increasingly unlikely.

Whether he intended to stay for good, or just for now, Best returned to Australia in 1990 with Mary Shatila for another go at the speaking, coaching and charity match circuit. And this time, he brought Denis Law with him.

Law was an early hero and an example for Best when he was coming through at United. Law was brought home to the English First Division from Torino in 1962. He became an irrepressible presence in the box for United, scoring key goals and generally tormenting opposition defenders. He was tall and charming with a thick shock of blond hair. As a media performer, there was a lot of Best in his ability to charm and he was always good for a one-liner.

Law had always symbolised *the professional* to Best. He was effortlessly lethal on the pitch, and the perfect finisher for a team with a lot of creative flair. And Best connected with Law very early on at United, even before he was in the first team. In the words of biographer Duncan Hamilton:

"As he mopped the dressing rooms, tidied kit and did odd jobs, Best spied on Law and noted his tousled blond hair, his worldly air and immaculate suits. Law looked like the 'modern-day Viking', he said."

In 1990, Law was coming to play the straight man to Best's ever declining sideshow.

But the tour started positively for both Best and Law, and Best had a chance to relive his mostly successful 1989 tour. Billy Millen had agreed to help organise the rest of the tour.

Best even repeated his interest in making Australia a new home to Australian press.

"I might end up living six months here and six months in America [with his son Calum]."

Then Best upped the ante by adding:

"I'd like to get a full-time coaching job with one of the professional teams here. If it could work out, it'd be terrific."

For this 1990 tour, Best told reporters soon after he arrived that he was inspired to return to Australia after an experience at a hospital visit the previous year. He was visiting patients at Lidcombe Hospital and encountered a fellow Belfast man whose 21-year-old son named Robert —a 'soccer nut'—was in a car accident and had not moved for two and a half months. Best then offered the young man a football that he had been carrying, and said to him, "You'd better put this under your sheets."

According to Best, Robert then moved his hand for the first time in months and slid the ball next to him under the sheets.

"I'm from Belfast and I've seen a lot of hardships," Best told reporters. "But it really got to me because I got a reaction from him."

So, when Best received a call in 1990 from Lidcombe Hospital to appear in a fundraiser match to purchase new video diagnostic equipment, he was quick to accept. And in a rather presumptuous move by the hospital, they asked Best to see if Denis Law would join him.

Oh, and twelve months on, Robert had recovered to the point where he would be able to kick-off the match: a George Best XI vs the Denis Law XI to be played as a curtain raiser to a Sydney Olympic vs West Adelaide curtain raiser, with Best suiting up to play. Law, who was 49, would coach from the sidelines.

A few days later, Best was reminded of the seedy nature of the Australian press when a piece in the light side of the Sydney Morning Herald reported on Best and Law's forthcoming coaching clinics with the Canterbury Girls High School football team.

"And in case you have a vision of the wild man from Northern Ireland roaming in the mud with eleven 16-year-olds, he is being accompanied by his girlfriend (Shatila),

LAW AND DISORDER (1990)

to whom he is most dearly attached."

Just why this was considered funny or appropriate can only be attributed to 'another time', but these are the sorts of *Carry On* football takes that Best could not avoid.

While seriously contemplating relocating (semi) permanently to Australia, it was a reminder of 1983's treatment that Best didn't need.

But this also wasn't the same Best who had put on a show wherever he went in 1983 or 1989. Even the presence of Law wasn't enough to elevate him. On the 1990 tour—sometimes referred to as the 'Best and Law Show'—Law often played Odin to Best's Loki.

Best's four tours of Australia each represent a phase of Best's descent into alcoholism. In 1967, he was not a drinker, and was on such a professional high that he did not need an artificial one. In 1983, he had chosen sobriety and tried to take a handle of his problem. In 1989, he drank, but more often than not he pulled it together when he needed to be somewhere. But in 1990, he just couldn't be relied on.

First, Best didn't appear at a sportsmen's night in Waverley. It was a 400-guest affair that Law ended up doing on his own. Then, shockingly, 48 hours later, he didn't appear for the Lidcombe Hospital charity match.

This was the very game that Best spoke so warmly and earnestly about. How he was moved by the patients, especially 'soccer nut' Robert, and how impactful his experience at the hospital had been in 1989. And still Best did not appear.

It's unclear from reports whether Robert was well enough to make the kick-off for the game which went ahead anyway without Best. But of all the people let down by Best that night, Robert was at the top of the list.

Law, who was on that list too, appeared pitch side and managed his team amiably.

The media at the time did not speculate why Best didn't appear, but their undertones of his drinking were clear. Later in the tour, Best added his own words to what was being whispered about him.

"People are saying it has all happened because of my drinking, but that is not a problem for me anymore. I can handle it."

Clearly this was untrue. In a fitting tribute, Waverley donated Best's speaking fee to Lidcombe Hospital, who also raised $3,600 on the day from donations.

Millen was incensed with Best.

"Coming on top of what happened the other night, this is too much," he told the press. The press then hinted at a possible dispute over future fees for Best, and a figure of $30,000 that Best was threatening legal action against Millen over.

Best was also a no-show at a coaching clinic at Parklea, west of Sydney, leaving 100 kids (whose parents had fronted $55) in the lurch. Luckily Socceroo captain Charlie Yankos was on hand to run the clinic with Law, and to stick around to offer autographs to the kids. Reporter Mike Cockerill was quick to add that more kids queued for Yankos' autographs than Law's, which was an odd expression of football pride given that Law had retired before any child in the queue under 16 was born.

The tour was descending rapidly. The Adelaide leg of the tour was cancelled, devastating fans who had spent $30 on a three course lunch in Best at the Travelodge Hotel and 350 would-be attendees of the sold-out speaking night at the Salsbury United Soccer club. A mooted exhibition game featuring Best on Salisbury United's pitch before the event also didn't go ahead.

Bookings in Melbourne did not steady the ship.

In Melbourne, football journalist Michael Lynch remembers one early Best 'appearance' with regret.

"[Best] was drunk at his speaking function and his language would make them blush on the Stretford End. Law, as he did many times for United, saved the day. Smart, sociable and a top speaker, he looked after his teammate that night, but could not help the Irishman giving Australia a first-hand look at his wild temper.

"One of the punters, who looked like he had as much to drink as Best, tried to convince the legend to dance with his wife. Best was having none of it, but the drunk persisted and then took offence and gave Best a piece of his mind. The Ulsterman responded by giving the drunk a piece of his fist."

At that point, Denis Law came in to save the day and wheeled Best out of the venue.

On this tour, the lessons Millen learned in the ceiling of the Marconi club seemed to leave him. One of the venues Millen booked bounced their $9,000 appearance cheque.

While Law was doing an adequate job of holding the tour together on stage, Millen had less than complimentary memories of him off stage.

"Denis Law wouldn't go anywhere. He wouldn't do anything. All he'd done was moan. It was the worst thing I could have done. Shocking. Just wouldn't mix with anybody. He shouldn't have come, you know. He just moaned the whole time."

Sydney reporters got a taste of Law's moods, when he, according to Ian Cockerill of the Sydney Morning Herald, "facetiously told of his delight at having to get out of bed at 5.30am to keep a noon rendezvous with the Sydney Press."

So, while Law wasn't having the greatest of times reopening old grievances, Best occasionally pulled it together for the one thing he really enjoyed: coaching clinics.

At Frankston Pines Soccer Club, Best ran a clinic with South Melbourne legend Paul Trimboli for the Victorian State under 15 side. Millen bet Best $20 in front of the kids that he couldn't hit the crossbar from forty yards.

"Bang! Right on to the post. I said, 'Who do you think you are, Georgie Best?'"

While in Melbourne, Best sought to re-energise the narrative of him permanently moving to Australia, and spruiked various business deals that he had in place.

He told Melbourne's *The Sun* that he was opening a business called 'George Best

Sports Design' to be located on Punt Road. He also reiterated his desire to coach a club in the NSL. To Best, it made a lot of sense: he had always enjoyed coaching kids and (for now) had such an affinity for the country that he was contemplating permanently moving to Australia. If it was good enough for his hero Ferenc Puskás, it was good enough for Best.

"We have formed a company in Melbourne so the incentive is there to be based here, and as long as the job appeals, I certainly would be interested in looking at it."

Nothing came of Best's 'offer' to coach in the NSL. It's also unclear if George Best Sports Design ever officially opened its doors to the public. Like so many of Best's endeavours, it was simply too good to be true.

While in Melbourne, Ken Morton crossed Bass Strait to meet up with Best again and organise another exhibition game. This time, Best would represent the 'Wrest Point Hotel Casino XI' against a 'British Airways World XI' at Morton's new coaching home of Olympia in Hobart.

Best and Law did a couple of speaking nights in Tassie beforehand which were memorable this time for different reasons.

"They forgot to advertise it," claims Millen. Only six people showed up for the second night.

The game in Hobart was similar to the year before, including Morton playing alongside Best again. David Crosson was also selected for the opposition again, but he was on his best behaviour. Law didn't play. He told reporters he hadn't played a minute of football since retiring in 1974—but he was manager of the British Airways side.

It was a massive success. Fans flocked to see Best for the last time, including Walter Pless who again covered the game for the local media. Best didn't hit the heights of 1989, with Pless describing his output as "showing little of the brilliance he exhibited last year".

Today, some fans report Best scoring a header from a corner while sitting on the shoulders of a teammate. In Pless' report, Best did find the back of the net, but under more charitable circumstances. When British Airways were awarded a penalty at the death, they let Best (playing for the other team) take it. His goal made it 8-7.

Morton remembers:

"The one in Hobart I played left back because he played left wing so that I could get the ball to him. The only thing I remember was I had to go into both dressing rooms at half-time and explain to people that nobody had come to watch [the rest of] them from the full 5,000-plus crowd. They came to watch Bestie. Give him the ball and let him play."

But despite pulling it together for the Tasmanian leg, behind the scenes the Best and Law tour had become a farce. Millen cancelled the tour early with a week left on the itinerary.

"The whole tour has been an utter disaster," Millen told the press. "I've decided to pull the plug."

Millen withheld the final $18,000 that Best was owed on the tour (from the contracted $30,000), principally for his non-attendance at events. Law pocketed the full amount owed to him—which was coincidentally $18,000 and much less than Best was due to earn.

On his way out, Best gave reporters a rather erroneous lesson in contract law:

"Everyone has mentioned the things I didn't attend, but what about all the functions I did go to?"

His final act was to underline how sour the relationship with Millen had become.

"It is easy to forgive enemies, but it is impossible to forgive friends when they say nasty things about you. I am very disappointed with the way things have happened, and the fact is Billy [Millen] and I are no longer on speaking terms."

Millen was also quoted in the press telling Best to "Go to hell".

After he had returned to London, Best was asked about his failed commitments on the tour by a reporter. Best's defence was that he was simply living his best life. "[Millen] caught me lying beside my swimming pool with a bottle of Dom Perignon and a dozen oysters at three in the afternoon on a 35-degree summer's day."

This was Best finally embracing the character journalists were hoping would alight at Mascot airport in 1983.

Best's final tour was also the final straw for Millen in the promotional tour business. Before the Best and Law tour, Millen told the press he was considering future tours with Bobby Moore and Pat Jennings. But after this Best tour had gone so poorly, his heart wasn't in it.

It was a common trend in Best's life that echoed in Australia. Most of his professional relationships that lasted longer than a charity match or a couple of speaking nights had a use-by date. There were only so many letdowns that the people in his orbit could bear. Clearly, his more successful 1989 tour represented more the exception than the norm for the increasingly erratic Best.

But just like Angie and Bill McMurdo, Billy Millen harboured no resentment towards Best. All those who held a long-term relationship with Best remember the warm and charismatic Best who was also capable of disappointment. The real Best, their friend, they carry in their hearts.

Best continued to play in exhibition games right up until the late 1990s, as many as 15 or 20 games a season, until his alcohol-affected health no longer permitted it.

The Final Act (1991-2005)

As 1990 ended, there was another turning point in Best's life that today represents his final descent. In September, he did his now infamous *Wogan* interview where a clearly drunk Best slurred for minutes before volunteering to host Terry Wogan that he likes "screwing".

'The Wogan Interview' became instantly infamous and led to an investigation into who allowed Best on air in that state. Little did the producers and backroom staff of *Wogan* know that one of Best's superpowers was that he could consume vast quantities of alcohol, seem completely sober, and then suddenly—in this case walking from the green room to the set—not be.

General media opportunities dried up after *Wogan*, but Best was still in demand as a football pundit. In between the odd appearance on the pitch, he worked as an analyst for LBC Radio during the Premier League era, as well as making an occasional appearance on Sky. He wove media punditry gigs in between still being the hottest ticket for emirs and billionaires to book for coaching clinics or sportsmen's nights.

By now, his occupation had moved into the 'football advisor' phase, or at least he was able to list that on his passport.

While Best the showman left hearts racing across Australia, the real impact of Best the football import didn't lead to an upsurge of interest in the Brisbane Lions, or the NSL, or at any club he played for across the country. While he represented a good payday, he wasn't the magic pill that the sport needed to add legitimacy or stir up lasting interest in the Australian club scene.

But to be fair to Best, nobody could. Sir Bobby Charlton and Kevin Keegan also flew into NSL crowds of 15,000 and then disappeared without a trace.

The crowds who flocked to Manchester United's tour in 1967 were totemic of the love of football that exists in Australia. Big British clubs like United, Liverpool or Celtic have always drawn crowds. And so, with that logic, Australian clubs have turned to these clubs for guest stars. Best, Charlton and Dwight Yorke on the United side, whereas Liverpool fans were given chances to see Keegan, Ian Rush, Ian Callaghan, Ray Clemence, Peter Beardsley, Robbie Fowler, Jimmy Case and Luis Garcia, not to mention local products Craig Johnston and Harry Kewell.

But that was never enough to make them stay. And so Australian clubs, largely to this day in the A-League, remain four-figure pulling draws.

In 1983, Best's treatment by the media also made it clear that he could not outrun his roguish alter-ego. In the press, he was a waste of money, washed up, a drunkard: and in moments when he was none of those things, he was a disappointment on the pitch.

There was never recognition of Best the man trying to find solid ground again on a pitch. Of the man who electrified crowds in 1967, and who in his day was capable of magic.

He had entered the Lions den seeking forgiveness through football, the one thing he was capable of producing. But instead, he was forced to remain in the shadow of his off-field baggage.

So, he did not inspire the local club scene like David Beckham conjured for Major League Soccer (MLS) in the US. He did not kick-off a Lions run that ended in a title or Cup win. He didn't score a forty-yard chip that is still discussed in hushed tones on the terraces.

At best, George's legacy in Australia is found in the relationships he built and reconnected while in the country. It is in the names like Ken Morton and David Jack, who still play an influential role in the sport.

Best was not an alien from planet football who landed on Redlands. He was a footballer in a time when football didn't create multi-millionaires, and his relationships with the sport underline how significant the sport has always been in Australia.

We are closer to the rest of the football world than we realise. We are, and always were, connected even if the threads are fragile, knotted or get burned at times.

The final act of Best's life was a tragic one. His redemption would not come through medical intervention or any religious awakening. He was always warmly welcomed back to Old Trafford as a guest, and his legend on the pitch grew through the Premier League era as Manchester United became a dominant force. And young Ryan Giggs with his electric pace, elite balance and knack for big goals would often provoke memories of Best on the terraces and the football media.

He also continued to work in the media. Even as his health deteriorated, he still found punditry work, mostly on Sky Sports, where his quick wit and passion for attacking, exciting football were embraced by fans.

The greatest compliments to Best often come from his fellow players, and especially teammates. Brian Kidd, who played and scored goals alongside Best during the peak of his career, remembers Best as a wizard on the pitch that he was often in awe of.

"I have been fortunate in being involved with coaching and playing in what must

THE FINAL ACT (1991-2005)

be close to 40-50 years ... I have been very lucky to have been around some great, world-class players."

And for Kidd, Best was right at the top of the tree.

"In my opinion, George, given the size of him, it wasn't just his technical ability, his heart was as big as a dustbin lid, so tough. He could tackle like a great defender, his range of passing short and long and obviously his dribbling and technical skills were out of this world. He was the best in the world."

By 2000, his liver was only functioning at 20%, and he was given a controversial liver transplant. By 2003, he was drinking again, and in late 2005 Best died aged 59 after the pills he was taking to accept the new liver failed and poisoned his kidneys. He was buried in Belfast in a state ceremony, with 100,000 brothers and sisters and world football's elite lining the streets to see him off.

"Just remember me for my football," was Best's final request shortly before he died.

Billy Millen, a Linfield legend who took on and conquered Manchester City at Windsor Park, and rodent infestations at Marconi, also sadly passed away in 2020 after a long illness.

Today Best is memorialised across Belfast. The city's airport is named after him. And Best's legacy has poignancy in Australia as it has worldwide. His performances in Australia perfectly mirror his stage of life each time and the trajectory of his career.

In 1967, he was touching greatness, and dazzled for the thousands who came to see him. In 1983, he was rehabilitating his image, but he did what he promised. He pulled crowds and created invaluable football memories for fans on the hills and grandstands. In 1989 and 1990, he was a version of himself—the version he was able to assemble in front of crowds (when he did manage to appear). When he was 'on', he was remarkable. And when he was off, or not present, he let everyone down.

And in matches in Australia, maybe he did stand on his teammates' shoulders to head-in a goal or steal the ball off his own teammates to go on a 40-yard run. Whether any of his more fanciful exploits happened or not doesn't matter. He was George Best, a legend in their midst, and in the years since, fantastical tales were bound to merge with fact.

Best's legend can be both sober and drunk at the same time, a sunk cost and worth every penny, a dazzling star and a dead weight in the midfield, scoring tap-ins and screamers. All of these are true of Best.

He was both an angel and fallen idol. And of all the legends to play in Australia, he was Best.

George Best's Games in Australia

1967

Friendlies
Manchester United 7 – Queensland 0 (Brisbane Exhibition Ground, Brisbane, June 4, 1967). Best goals: 2
Manchester United 3 – Sydney Representative XI 0 (Sydney Showgrounds, Sydney, June 7, 1967). Best goals: 2
Manchester United 1 – Victoria XI 1 (Olympic Park, Melbourne, June 11, 1967).
Manchester United 3 – Northern New South Wales 0 (Newcastle Sports Ground, Newcastle, June 12, 1967). Best goals: 2
Manchester United 3 – New South Wales 1 (Sydney Showgrounds, Sydney, June 18, 1967).
Manchester United 4 – Victorian State League XI 0 (Olympic Park, Melbourne, June 21, 1967). Best goals: 1
Manchester United 5 – South Australia 1 (Kensington Oval, Adelaide, June 24, 1967).
Manchester United 7 – Western Australia 0 (WACA, Perth, June 27, 1967).
Best goals: 3

1983

League Games
Brisbane Lions 2 – Sydney Olympic 1 (Perry Park, Brisbane, July 3, 1983).
Brisbane Lions 0 – St George 3 (Perry Park, Brisbane, July 8, 1983).
Marconi 1 – Brisbane Lions 1 (Marconi Stadium, Sydney, July 10, 1983).
Brisbane Lions 0 – Adelaide City 4 (Richlands Stadium, Brisbane, July 17, 1983).
Osborne Park Galeb 2 – 1 Melville Alemmania (Perth, July 24, 1983).
Best goals: 1

Friendlies

West Adelaide 5 – Adelaide City 3 (Hindmarsh Stadium, Adelaide, July 20, 1983).
    Best goals: 1
Dee Why 2 – Manly- Warringhah 3 (Cromer Park, Sydney, July 27, 1983).
    Best goals: 1

1989

Friendlies

Celebrity XI 5 – Australian XI 2 (Doncaster Rovers Soccer Club, Melbourne,
    June 18, 1989). Best goals: 3
Devonport City XI 2 –- Tasmania XI 2 (Valley Road, Devonport, 6 July 6, 1989).
Sam Service XI 6 - George Best XI 6 (Ramsay Park, Elizabeth, 23 July 1989).
    Best Goals: 1

1990

Friendlies

Wrest Point Hotel Casino XI 7 – British Airways World XI 8
    (South Hobart Oval, Hobart, February, 1990). Best goals: 1

Bibliography and Related Sources

This book was inspired by Lucas and Jason's first book together, *Be My Guest – Football Superstars in Australia* (Fair Play Publishing, 2021). Some sections of this book are contained in *Be My Guest – Football Superstars in Australia*.

The following books, newspapers, magazines and websites were used in the research for this book.

Docherty, Tommy, *The Doc: Hallowed Be Thy Game*, Headline Publishing Group, 2006

Best, George, *Blessed: The Autobiography*, Ebury Press, 2002

Hamilton, Duncan, *Immortal: The Biography of George Best*, Windmill Books, 2014

These Football Times

Ozfootball.net

Melbournesoccer.blogspot.com

Cherry Chimes (afcbchimes.blogspot.com)

Parkinson in Australia (Channel 10)

Sportscene (Channel 7)

Soccer Action

Soccer World

Soccer International

Sydney Morning Herald

TheWorldGame.sbs.com.au

Manutd.com

Australian Soccer Weekly

Dailymail.co.uk

Goal.com

Theblizzard.co.uk

The Guardian

The Age

Smfc.com.au

BIBLIOGRAPHY AND RELATED SOURCES

Independent.co.uk
Soccer News
Soccer Federation of Western Australia Yearbook
David Jack's Blog: djcjack.com
ABC News
Walter Pless' Blog: walterplessonsoccer.blogspot.com
The *Courier Mail*
The Belfast Telegraph
Fulhamish podcast

A special thank you to the following people for their guidance, support and content in putting this book together.

Firstly, thanks to Bill McMurdo, who was extremely generous with his time and memories of his dear former friend. Bill's accounts were essential to fill in the many gaps in the archives of Australian football news. It was a gift to spend an afternoon with Bill and reflect on George's life and impact on the game.

Thank you also to Brian and Gemma Kidd. Brian Kidd is one of football's true gentlemen, was very generous with his time, and Australian football fans are honoured that his emergence into the United side first happened on our pitches.

Massive thanks also to David Jack, Gary James, John O'Connell, John Bennett, Ken Morton, Henk Mollee, Mike Mulvey and Nigel Lownds who were all fantastic resources and central characters in Best's Australian story. Their memories of playing with and against Best, as well as (in Mollee's case) the role he played in signing Best, made this book possible. Crucially, Best was a recurring theme in their football lives which really helped demonstrate the 'through line' between Australia and football's superstars.

And to Billy Millen. Millen sadly passed away about a year after our interview. He was extremely warm, hilariously funny and—like my other interviewees—his company was a joy. He represents one of many football pioneers in Australia whom we are gradually losing from the historical accounts. Without the opportunity to speak with Billy, Best's full Australian story could not have been told.

Thanks also to Andrew Howe, West Adelaide SC, Evan Morgan Grahame, Michael Lynch, Mark Boric, Vicky Morton, Grantlee Kieza, Cliff Pointer, Walter Pless, Robbie Slater and our publisher, Bonita Mersiades of Fair Play Publishing.

About the Authors

Jason and Lucas crossed paths whilst playing cricket together for Richmond City Cricket Club. Social media saw them understand they both shared a passion for the Socceroos and enjoyed the quirky history of Australian football.

Jason and Lucas first worked together on *Be My Guest – Football Superstars in Australia* (2021, Fair Play Publishing).

Be My Guest was brainstormed together on the nine-hour drive from Melbourne to Jamberoo, New South Wales, for the inaugural Australian Football Writers' Festival in 2019.

Jason has also written *Surfing for England* (2019) and *Green and Golden Boots* (2023), both published by Fair Play Publishing.

MORE REALLY GOOD FOOTBALL BOOKS FROM FAIR PLAY PUBLISHING

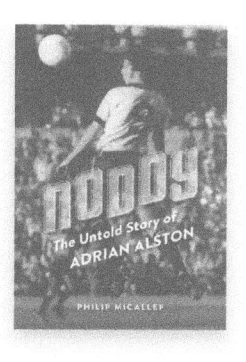

Available from
fairplaypublishing.com.au/shop
and all good bookstores

FAIRPLAY
PUBLISHING

www.fairplaypublishing.com.au

Milton Keynes UK
Ingram Content Group UK Ltd.
UKHW022101290324
440241UK00007B/335